Salute to the LNER

G. FREEMAN ALLEN

LONDON
IAN ALLAN LTD

First published 1977

ISBN 0 7110 0789 6

Published by Ian Allan Ltd, Shepperton, Surrey, and printed in the United Kingdom by Ian Allan Printing Ltd.

By the same author
Railways the World Over
British Railways Today and Tomorrow
British Rail After Beeching

Contents

4463

The LNER is Born

Second largest of the pre-nationalisation 'Big Four' railways, the London & North Eastern was a company of considerable and varied achievements. It made the world record books with a steam speed peak that will never be surpassed, put up by a class of engine that was daily running Britain's fastest train. It built Britain's biggest passenger locomotive, its biggest freight locomotive and its most efficient express passenger locomotive. One of its constituent companies, the Great Northern, had been in the van of passenger travel improvement with the first British dining car, in 1879. The LNER continued the pioneering — sometimes with lasting success, as with electric cooking on trains; at other times with marks for a brave try the only entry in British railway history, as with its experiments in on-train radio and cinema, the 'Flying Scotsman's' hairdressing saloon and cocktail bar, and its sleepers with showerbaths.

The LNER could trace its origins right back to railways' birthplace, the North-East of England. By 1820 the coalfields of Northumberland and Durham were already criss-crossed by over 200 miles of horse-operated wagonways. Then an enterprising young colliery engineer, George Stephenson, persuaded the promoters of the Stockton & Darlington Railway to adopt locomotive power; and on September 27, 1825, the S&DR was inaugurated as the world's first public passenger- and freight-carrying railway worked by steam traction.

Within a decade the North Eastern railway promoters were striking southwards to London. The first through route was finished as early as 1840, but it was a circuitous one from York via Church Fenton, Normanton, Chesterfield and Derby to Euston. A year later trains were running north of York to Darlington and by 1844 to the Gateshead area of Newcastle via Washington (the direct Team Valley rtute via Durham was not complete until 1872); by 1847 tracks had been driven beyond Newcastle to Tweedmouth. The final gaps in a through railway to Scotland were closed with completion of Robert Stephenson's handsome bridges over the Tyne and Tweed, the ironwork High Level Bridge at Newcastle in the autumn of 1849 and the brickwork Royal Border Bridge at Berwick in the summer of 1850.

Left: In garter blue livery, class A4 4-6-2 No 4463 *Sparrow Hawk* storms London's Northern Heights in the late 1930s with the 16.00 Kings Cross, Leeds and Bradford express./*Eric Treacy*

Most of the companies principally involved in this expansion merged in 1854 as the North Eastern Railway. At that date the NER was the most extensive railway in Britain, with 720 route-miles of track. In the next 69 years it was to become the biggest, the richest and the most influential of the companies that formed the LNER in 1923. Not only did it cater for a territory with generous natural resources in coal, ore and limestone, which stimulated a great deal of heavy industry demanding bulk transport, but its tight network touched important ports and navigable rivers — in fact, the NER also became the largest dock-owner of the pre-1923 companies. And in bidding for the freight tonnage thrown up by this industrial environment the NER had an advantage shared by none of the major pre-1923 freight-carrying railways: a monopoly of practically its entire area.

The Stockton & Darlington, which did not join the NER until 1863, brought on to the NER map its most spectacular freight lines. The NER's constituent companies had pushed some remarkable railways high into the hills of Durham and Yorkshire to get at the territory's ore, but two of the highest-climbing — to 1,474ft above sea level at Parkhead, west of Durham, and to 1,370ft at Burton Head, in the Cleveland Hills south of Middlesbrough — used rope haulage for their steepest pitches. The third, though, faced steam power with the highest standard-gauge railway summit in England.

This was the line sponsored by the S&D from West Auckland and Barnard Castle over the Pennines to Kirkby Stephen and Tebay, to open up a route for the Cumbrian and Lancashire haematite which the Durham ironfounders needed as leaven for ore from the Cleveland Hills to enhance their product. Opened in 1861, this cross-country line clambered up the wild fells on long grades as steep as 1 in 60 to a height of 1,378ft at Stainmore summit. On the way it soared over valleys on some striking bridgework, especially the spindly, latticework Belah Viaduct, 1040ft long and 196ft high, designed and built by Sir Thomas Bouch, who went on to create the disastrous first Tay Bridge. Winter was savage on the Stainmore line and on several occasions its trains were stranded for days in huge snowdrifts. After World War II its freight traffic declined and it was shut down in 1961.

But though freight was the backbone of its business, the NER had a reputation with its passengers too. For years it timetabled Britain's fastest train over the 44.1mile Darlington-York 'racetrack'. It was also the first British railway outside London to apply electric traction to suburban traffic, running electric trains over a section of the North Tyneside lines around Newcastle by the end of March, 1904, just a week ahead of the Lancashire & Yorkshire Railway's inauguration of electric operation between Liverpool and Southport.

The Great Northern Railway made contact with the NER in 1849. First the massive GNR project, envisaging a Peterborough-Boston-Lincoln-Doncaster loop as well as a direct main line, had to contend with a rival scheme to project the Eastern Counties Railway northward from Cambridge as the main London-York railway. The ECR, in fact, was already on the way with an extension through Cambridge and Ely to Peterborough, opened in 1846. But Parliament swallowed the GNR proposal, the 327 route-miles of which made up the biggest single new railway proposal ever laid before it. By 1849 the GNR had gained Doncaster via its Lincolnshire loop (construction of which was given precedence over the direct line), then the existing Manchester, Sheffield & Lincolnshire Railway line across country from Lincoln to Retford, and thence over its own new line into Doncaster. The GNR had also built beyond Doncaster to Askern, whence it could run to Leeds over Lancashire & Yorkshire and Midland Railway metals successively, until in 1866 it finished its own route to Leeds via Wakefield.

By the middle of the last century the GNR had today's London-Doncaster main line operational throughout. Trains were travelling from Peterborough to London in August, 1850, at first to a temporary station at Maiden Lane, but to the newly-opened Kings Cross from October, 1852. In August, 1852 the direct 'Towns' line from Peterborough over Stoke Summit to Grantham and Retford was finished.

North of Doncaster, though, trains between London and the North-East still had to meander through Knottingley and Church Fenton to reach York, and via Leamside and Penshaw to gain Newcastle for almost two more decades. At last the direct Doncaster-Selby-York line was ready in January 1871. With it came other important new connections and changes in the York area. Until then through trains had been compelled to reverse in the old York station, a terminus just inside the ancient City wall on the east side of the present-day route; this could now be abandoned — in

Below: The first rail bridge over the Tyne at Newcastle, the High Level, with an ex-NER Class G5 0-4-4T passing a Tyneside electric of the final LNER North Tyneside pattern; in the left background is a Class V2 2-6-2./*E R Wethersett*

Top right: The Royal Border Bridge, Berwick, with an ex-NER Class B14 4-6-0 heading a southbound express over the Tweed./*Ian Allan Library*

Centre right: Durham Viaduct, with Durham cathedral in the background./*Ian Allan Library*

Bottom right: A post-nationalisation view of Belah Viaduct, on the Kirkby Stephen-Penrtih line, with two BR Class 3 2-6-0s crossing at the head of a summer Saturday Blackpool-Newcastle train in 1955./*J. W Armstrong*

later years it was converted to a carriage depot — and traffic could pass straight through the striking new station, with its curving arched roof.

As already mentioned, the Team Valley main line via Durham came into use in 1872. The last obstacle to straightforward East Coast main-line operation was not removed until 1906, when reversal at Newcastle was obviated by the opening of the King Edward VII bridge further up the Tyne, allowing down trains to enter Newcastle Central station from the south, instead of coming in to face south off the High Level Bridge from Gateshead.

The GNR's outstanding monument today is, naturally, the East Coast main line. Its Lincolnshire network has withered somewhat in a road transport age and BR rationalisation has concentrated London-Sheffield and Manchester traffic on the Midland, though for a few post-1948 years the Eastern Region was allowed to run the fastest London-Sheffield service out of Kings Cross as a reminder of earlier GNR enterprise in this direction, using the MS&L line from Retford to the steel city. Another important GNR extension was from Grantham westwards into direct competition with the Midland for coal tonnage from the Leen and Erewash valleys of the Nottinghamshire coalfield.

First of the LNER's constituents to build a main line out of London was the Great Eastern Railway's precursor, the Eastern Counties Railway. The ECR had penetrated to Romford from its original London terminus of Bishopsgate by June, 1839. It struggled as far as Colchester by 1843, but there it wilted, exhausted by the cost of railway-building within London and of tackling the clay uplands beyond Brentwood. What time another company (later taken over by the ECR) carried on through Ipswich to Norwich and reached the latter city in December 1849, the ECR switched to easier-looking schemes aiming at Norwich via Cambridge and Ely; these projects took shape as a through route in July, 1845.

From the two London-Norwich arteries, the projection from Ely to Peterborough noted earlier, and offshoots into East Anglia and to its coastline, the Great Eastern Railway was born by mergers in 1862.

Eventually Liverpool Street — built at enormous cost in the late 1860s and opened piecemeal in 1874-5 — did become another London terminus for York and beyond. In 1879-82 the GNR and GER agreed on joint operation of the line from March to Doncaster via Spalding, Sleaford, Lincoln and Gainsborough, and with the grant of running powers beyond Doncaster by the NER the GER was able to operate a daily Liverpool Street-York express service. Immediately prior to World War I the 11.05 from Liverpool Street was taking 5hr 20 min over this circuitous city-to-city journey.

East Anglia was no treasure-house of traffic and the GER's anxiety to tap the North-South traffic was prompted by its chronic poverty. Shortage of cash drove it to economise in construction, so that it left the ER a heritage of weight-restricted bridges and curvature that inhibited production of locomotives with power in reserve for its heavy holiday coast trains until BR came up with the 'Britannia' Pacifics. The GER stimulated the close-packed development of the North-East London suburbs, but could not raise the wind for essential electrification of the network; instead, it was forced in 1920 to put on the world's most intensive steam-operated train service, involving the peak-hour despatch or receipt at Liverpool Street of 24 trains in 60min over the same pair of metals. This fantastic operation, executed with stumpy little 0-6-0Ts and rakes of primitive, wooden-seated six-wheelers, averaged out at the provision of 350 passenger seats every minute. It is described more fully in Chapter Six.

The third of the LNER's main lines into London, the Great Central, was a latecomer. Founder of the enterprise was the Sheffield, Ashton-under-Lyne & Manchester Railway, which by the end of 1845 had thrust its 3mile Woodhead Tunnel — longest in Britain until 1886 — through the Pennines. The LNER eventually electrified this difficult route, with its long stretches of 1 in 100-120 gradient up to the tunnel, because of its importance as a coal carrier from the Yorkshire pits to Lancashire industry.

In 1847 the SA&M and two other companies merged as the Manchester, Sheffield & Lincolnshire. For more than 40 years thereafter the MS&L squeezed a bare living out of just a cross-country route linking Manchester and the East Coast ports of Grimsby and New Holland. But in the mid-1860s the company's chair was taken by one of the 19th Century's liveliest railway entrepreneurs, Sir Edward Watkyn. Chairman not merely of the Metropolitan and South Eastern Railway as well as the MS&L, but also of the Channel Tunnel company, he dreamed of presiding over one through route from the North to the French coast. And so, in the 1890s, one more trunk route was driven from the provinces to London.

Built at forbidding cost, the London Extension of

Above right: York station, seen from the south. The original terminus was to the right of the picture. In this late 1930s scene green-liveried Class A4 4-6-2 No 4493 *Woodcock* is disposing of the stock of a semi-fast from Newcastle./*Real Photographs*

Right: The down side at Kings Cross in the 1930s, with Class A1 4-6-2 No 2555 *Centenary* moving the 'Queen of Scots' out of Platform 10. To the right is the Suburban station, with the steeply graded exit from the Moorgate line climbing up to the right of the Pacific's exhaust./*Real Photographs*

Nº 4493

QUEEN OF SCOTS

the Great Central Railway, as the MS&L was renamed in 1897, reached the capital via Nottingham, Leicester and Rugby in 1898; a year later it was running passenger trains into a brand-new London terminus at Marylebone. Commercially, it was an absurd enterprise. The Great Central's lightweight expresses between Marylebone, the East Midlands, Bradford (via a branch from Penistone), Sheffield and Manchester — every one with refreshment car, GCR publicity stressed — won plaudits for comfort and smart operation, but never competed convincingly with the more direct routes of the old-established companies. The circuitousness of its routes equally handicapped the GCR's freight salesmen, though with the aid of a branch from Woodford Halse to the GWR at Banbury it did attract a considerable tonnage of Midlands-South-West freight away from the congested Birmingham area.

But the GCR's sanguine shareholders never sniffed a dividend. After World War II BR allowed the passenger service a few years' infusion of named trains and special promotion, but then withdrew benevolence and left the service to rot to a near-standstill. At length, in September 1966, the crumbling remains of the Great Central main line were shut down all the way from the London Transport border at Aylesbury to the outskirts of Sheffield.

The East Coast Route's partner in Scotland, the North British, commanded the south-eastern quarter of the country. It opened from Edinburgh to Berwick in 1846, and by its own new construction and absorption of other companies built up Scotland's largest rail system by the end of the 19th Century. From Edinburgh Waverley, the country's most handsome station, the NBR radiated to Dundee and Aberdeen, to Berwick, to Carlisle over the Waverley Route, to Glasgow over the most direct route between the two cities; and from Glasgow's suburban outskirts it operated after 1908 the superbly scenic West Highland line to Fort William, opened in 1894 and pushed on to the coast at Mallaig in 1901.

For many years Edinburgh-Dundee-Aberdeen through passengers had to detrain into ferries to cross the broad Firths of Forth and Tay. The conjunction of poor groundwork, injudicious design and shoddy construction that wrecked the first Tay Bridge in a December gale of 1879, hurling a mail train and 79 people into the water, has been oft told. The present 2mile bridge, the longest on BR, was finished in 1887. After the Tay Bridge disaster, Bouch's plan for a mammoth suspension bridge over the Forth was discarded and between 1883 and 1890 the still breathcatching structure of today's Forth Bridge was assembled by a work-force that sometimes totalled 4,500. Each of its three towers is 330ft high, each of the two main spans 1,710ft long and its total length including approach viaducts just over 2 miles; its tracks are 157ft above the water.

The North British was another LNER constituent with substantial marine interests. Its elegant paddle-steamers plied up and down the Clyde from a pier adjoining Craigendoran station and it also shared ownership of the Loch Lomond steamers with the Caledonian Railway. Besides having a healthy rail traffic into and out of Scotland's East Coast ports, the NBR was itself a dock-owner — in fact, the most affluent of the Scottish railways in this respect.

The sparsely populated territory beyond Aberdeen was the bailiwick of the little Great North of Scotland Railway, which opened the first section of its 334 route-mile network in 1854. It bequeathed the LNER service of a second royal residence, Balmoral Castle, which was reached over the 43mile Ballater branch from Aberdeen, a single line which the GNoS operated as efficiently as any in the country. The other royal home to which the LNER ministered was, of course, Sandingham, served by Wolferton station on the Great Eastern's Kings Lynn-Hunstanton line.

One other company was virtually a Grouping entrant of the LNER, though it had actually amalgamated with the NER in 1922. This was the Hull & Barnsley, born in 1880 of Hull's disgruntlement with the NER and a conviction that the latter was diverting maritime traffic from Hull to Tees-side ports. A wasteful duplicate line 53miles long was driven inland, at high cost in earthworks, from a big and handsome new dock at Hull to a junction with the Midland Railway at Cudworth, near Barnsley, and from 1885 to 1899 the H&BR waged ruinous rate war on the NER. At the turn of the century Hull and the H&BR mended their fences with the NER, and from 1899 to 1914 the H&BR operated at a slender profit. Its move into the black was aided by a booming coal market, since its principal traffic was export coal from South Yorkshire pits to Hull docks. H&B passenger traffic was slight, though until World War I it did run its own Hull-Sheffield express service behind its own locomotives, using Midland tracks beyond Cudworth, in competition with the Great Central. As already remarked, the H&BR was given special consent to merge with the NER in advance of the 1923 Grouping, after which it steadily lost sense and usefulness. But not until the nationalised British Railways wielded the rationalising axe in earnest was it shut down, save

Above left: The Forth Bridge: one of the ex-GC 'Director' 4-4-0 batch specially built for Scotland after the Grouping, No 6389 *Haystoun of Bucklaw,* heads a stopping train./*Cecil J Allen collection*

Left: The Tay Bridge, longest in Britain: ex-NBR Atlantic No 9872 *Auld Reekie* heads for Edinburgh with an express from Aberdeen and Dundee./*Ian Allan Library*

for short lengths at each end of the original route, in 1959.

Several railways which pre-1923 companies had run in partnership remained joint operations within the post-Grouping Big Four. Most important of those in which the newly-formed LNER acquired an interest was the 143 route-mile Cheshire Lines Committee. The title was something of a misnomer, for the hub of the CLC was its Lancashire main line of 34 miles from Manchester Central to Liverpool Central, with a loop catering for Warrington and a branch to Southport, though it also had a branch to Chester. Originators of the CLC in 1865 were the Manchester, Sheffield & Lincolnshire and Great Northern Railways, joined by the Midland a year later; after 1923, therefore, the CLC became an LMS-LNER Joint Railway, with the LNER the senior partner, so that the line was operated with LNER coaching stock. Pre-1923 the CLC had its own coaching stock, but no motive power; Great Central engines hauled its trains, which featured one of Britain's first regular-interval services, an hourly shuttle between Liverpool and Manchester in 45min with a stop at Warrington.

Most picturesque beyond doubt of the Joint Railways in the LNER fold was the Midland & Great Northern. This was an amalgam of several small companies that mushroomed on the northern fringe of Great Eastern territory and combined forces in 1895, setting up headquarters at Kings Lynn. Eventually, under equal and joint management by the Midland and Great Northern Railways, the M&GN stretched across the East Midlands and East Anglia from an end-on junction with the Midland at Saxby, near Melton Mowbray, through Peterborough and Kings Lynn to Melton Constable, whence three arms extended to Sheringham and Cromer, Yarmouth and Norwich.

The M&GN was entirely self-contained, with its own locomotives and rolling stock, overhauled in its own workshops at Melton Constable; some of its engines were derivatives or straight copies of its parent Midland and GN designs, but others — notably its charming outside-cylinder 4-4-0s — were attractively

Below: The last main into London, the Great Central, running parallel with the Metropolitan Railway near Willesden Green: in this 1930s scene one of the Class B17 4-6-0s with short tender originally built for the GE line, No 2842 *Kilverstone Hall,* heads a Marylebone-Manchester express./*E R Wethersett. Ian Allan Library*

Below right: A Great North of Scotland Railway 4-4-0, LNER Class D40 No 6834; this was one of many pre-grouping 4-4-0 classes which the LNER blessed with green livery in the early years of the Grouping./*P Ransome-Wallis*

original. These little machines were often taxed to the limit by the sequence of heavy holiday trains funelled over the M&GN's single line at summer weekends; so was operating ingenuity. But for the rest of the year local passenger and agricultural business was thin gruel financially. The M&GN was a heavy money-loser and when nationalisation underlined the availability of alternative routes for cross-country traffic to the East Anglian towns and coastline it was axed. It was, in fact, the first secondary main line to be shut down: save for two or three short sections, the whole system was closed in February, 1959.

The other significant joint line shared by the LNER with another post-1923 company was the former GNR-LNWR connection from Bottesford, on the GN Grantham-Nottingham line, to the LNWR at Welham Junction, near Market Harborough. This system, aggregating 45 route miles with branches, gave the GNR access to its own passenger and goods stations at Leicester; conversely, the LNWR used to run passenger and freight traffic into Nottingham.

Such, then, was the constitution of LNER in outline. So dominant was the North Eastern Railway in almost every department — it had nearly twice the mileage, twice the staff, well over twice the vehicles, many more locomotives and twice the freight tonnage compared with the other member companies, besides making nearly twice the profit; only in passenger carrying did it yield premier place to the Great Eastern — that not surprisingly York was canvassed by many as the LNER headquarters city. In the end London's Liverpool Street offices were chosen, but the new LNER Board avoided over-centralisation. It instituted an Area management organisation that had a good deal of autonomy, except in such obvious matters for standardisation as rolling stock design and purchases. Each of the three Areas had its own advisory Board and the Scottish Area even its own General Manager, whereas those at the head of the North Eastern and Southern (covering ex-GC, GE and GN territory) Areas were less grandly titled Divisional General Managers.

One final point of interest — 'London & North Eastern' was far from being a unanimous choice of title for the new company. Some protested that it was just an unimaginative twist of 'London & North Western' and Southerners objected that it was over-emphasising the NER content of the system. Several Board Members urged a less ponderous title, not least to economise in the number of initials to be applied to the company's chattels, and there was powerful advocacy of 'Great North Railway' or 'North East Railway'. Ironically, LNER wagons were never lettered with more than a laconic 'NE'.

The Locomotive Inheritance

Unlike the rival LMS, the LNER opened its account with four-coupled engines hauling the majority of its expresses between London and the North. The NER had been beaten only by the Highland Railway in turning out Britain's first 4-6-0 tender engine. Its engineer Wilson Worsdell, younger of two brothers who successively managed NER mechanical affairs, had in 1899 and 1900 produced 6ft 1¼in and 6ft 8¼in driving wheel 4-6-0s that became LNER Classes B13 and B14. But their looks were more flattering than their performance. The small-wheeled B13s could not match the dash even of the NER Class R 4-4-0s (subsequently LNER D20) on East Coast expresses and though the B14s were a little more impressive, only five were built.

When Vincent Raven succeeded Worsdell in 1910, he reverted to 4-4-2s for express work. The B13s and B14s were lumped with the later NER 4-6-0 designs (LNER Classes B15 and B16) as mixed traffic engines. For the most part they wore express passenger headcode only on holiday reliefs and excursions, and the cream of the passenger work was handled by the elegant NER Atlantics, Worsdell's two-cylinder (LNER C6) and Raven's three-cylinder (LNER C7) types, supported by the better of the NER 4-4-0s.

Both Worsdell and Raven Atlantics lasted almost the whole life of the LNER, working chiefly from York, Gateshead, Heaton and Leeds Neville Hill sheds. Gradually Gresley's Pacifics ousted them from front-rank express work and in the 1930s his V2 2-6-2s completed the job, relegating the 4-4-2s to stopping passenger and brake-fitted freight jobs. But more than once one of the C7s stationed at Tweedmouth for fast freight work in the late 1930s had glory thrust back upon it when it was hurriedly commandeered to take over the 'Coronation' streamliner from an A4 Pacific that had failed on the Newcastle-Edinburgh stretch of its journey.

At the birth of the LNER, therefore, double-heading of East Coast expresses was rife north of York, since the NER's northern neighbour, the North British, bequeathed the LNER nothing bigger than an Atlantic. The stiff gradients on the NBR's routes from Edinburgh to Carlisle, Perth and Aberdeen cried out for a six-coupled engine (and the competing Caledonian had them), but the NBR locomotive engineer, W. P. Reid, was forced by his directors to defer to the civil engineer, who insisted on 4-4-2s. The NBR Atlantics were some of the most beautifully proportioned engines built in Britain, but lacklustre performers; all were scrapped between 1933 and 1939.

H. A. Ivatt's Atlantics, in contrast, were beyond a doubt the outstanding British 4-4-2s. Ivatt's first essay — and Britain's first 4-4-2 — was the lean, small-boilered type that was known as the 'Klondyke' because its 1898 emergence coincided with the celebrated Yukon Gold Rush. The 'Klondykes' (LNER Class C2) knew well the feel of 400ton East Coast expresses up to the 1920s and were not totally excluded from single-handed long-distance work until the advent of the Gresley V2 2-6-2s in the mid-1930s. Even then one could find them piloting a big Atlantic on express work at peak holiday periods, and they were conceded an Indian summer of speed on the inaugural Kings Cross-Cambridge 'Beer Trains' (see Chapter Four) at the start of the 1930s.

In their final, superheated form the large-boilered Class C1 Atlantics displayed capabilities almost incredible for engines with such relatively small cylinders and limited adhesion weight. More than once, for example, a C1 was timed to haul a 16coach load of more than 500tons from Grantham to York, 82.7miles, in only 87min, a feat which would have been regarded as above average if it had been recorded with a Pacific. Their pace on the Pullmans after the acceleration of the early 1930s (see Chapter Four) was equally impressive, though a driver needed a placid stomach to push an Ivatt Atlantic up to 90mph because of its often prodigious roll at speed.

As late as 1936 a C1 could still make Doncaster to London, 156miles, in 139min, as No.4452 did one day when it had to take over the 'Silver Jubilee' streamliner from an ailing A4. By then Pacifics were in command of the principal express passenger turns, but the Atlantics were standbys at the main stations south of York, hence their occasional opportunities to relive their past, which No.4452 seized so eagerly. Their last speed fling was on the Kings Cross-Cambridge 'Beer Trains' when the loads of these trains oustripped the

Above right: Ex-NER Class B16 4-6-0 No 931 heads a Leeds train out of York. The NER was notorious for its bewilderingly lavish signal gantries, like the example in this picture./*Real Photographs*

Right: One of Raven's Class C7 ex-NER 4-4-2s, No 2163, near Beningbrough with the Swansea-Newcastle through train (the centre of the train is an ex-GWR clerestory-roof coach set)./*Real Photographs*

931

T7955

capacity of other four-coupled types. World War II faced them once more with huge East Coast main loads which, coupled with scanty maintenance, left them decrepit when the peace came. Gradually, between 1943 and 1950, they were at last withdrawn from service.

Both GNR and NER had a Pacific in the wings on the eve of the Grouping. Nigel Gresley, appointed GNR locomotive chief in 1911 at the age of 35, was first in the arena. His No.1470 *Great Northern* of 1922, with its majestic lines, big high-pitched boiler tapering into a wide firebox, roomy and windowed cab, and stately eight-wheeled tender fully exploited the potential of the wheel arrangement. In designing it Gresley had intently studied the best Pacific practice abroad, especially on the US Pennsylvania Railroad. The GWR 4-6-2 *The Great Bear,* which had been running since 1908, had in contrast been essentially a Churchward 4-6-0 inflated to justify the longer wheelbase; and the same criticism could be levelled with even more force at the Pacific of the NER's motive power chief, Sir Vincent Raven, which was shaping on the drawing board as no more than an enlargement of his Atlantics.

Appointed Chief Mechanical Engineer of the new LNER, Gresley open-mindedly allowed construction of the Raven Pacifics to proceed, even though a 1923 summer trial of one of first two completed, No.2400 *City of Newcastle,* against his own A1 (the initial LNER classification of the Gresley 180lb boiler pressure prototype) was almost 'no contest'. The Raven engine's coal consumption was well in excess of the A1's, its overlong parallel boiler steamed indifferently and it was prone to overheat because of defective design detail. Rebuilding of one of the Raven quintet, No.2404 *City of Ripon,* with an A1 boiler did not materially improve performance and all five, the LNER's first Class A2, were scrapped in 1936-7.

The GNR it was, then, which handed the new-born

Below: A 'Klondyke', one of Ivatt's first small-boilered GN Atlantic series: Class C2 No 3255 pauses at Hadley Wood with a Hitchin-Kings Cross stopping train./*C R L Coles*

Right: Raven's NER Pacific: Class A2 No 2401 *City of Kingston Upon Hull* storms out of Edinburgh past Craigentinny with an up express in 1927./*P Ransome-Wallis*

Below right: The first Gresley Pacific in original condition, before boiler mountings and cab were reduced in height: No 4470 *Great Northern* tops Potters Bar summit with the 17.45 Kings Cross-West Riding express in 1928. On the down slow in the distance one can just make out the 'birdcage' brake of one of the North London four-wheeler sets that provided the Broad Street suburban services in those days./*F R Hebron*

2401

No 447

L M S

Nº 6104

LNER its principal express passenger power of the future. Gresley had confidently forecast that his new 4-6-2 would be able to tackle even 600ton loads on existing East Coast schedules, compared with the Atlantics' normal 300-400ton maxima. He quickly proved the point by having the second of the breed, No.1471, haul a 20coach, 617ton special from Kings Cross to Grantham, 105miles, on the then 120min booking of the 'Flying Scotsman'.

The Great Central's last mechanical chief, J. G. Robinson, had been dithering between four- and six-coupled designs for his principal power. His first 4-6-0 essay of 1902 was a mixed traffic type (LNER B5) with 6ft 1in wheels, locomotives known throughout their life as the 'Fish Engines' because the GCR promptly applied them to its cherished fast fish trains from Grimsby. But to meet a more powerful passenger engine requirement the following year Robinson hedged his bets by ordering simultaneously his first two 4-4-2s (the graceful LNER C4) and two 4-6-0s (LNER B1 until Thompson's mixed traffic 4-6-0 was thus classified, whereafter the GC engines became B18). The C4 and B1 were designed for conversion to 4-6-0 and 4-4-2 respectively should one or other arrangement prove markedly superior, but there was never any rebuilding; in fact, although Robinson at first opted to multiply his Atlantics, in 1906 he had 10 more 4-6-0s built, almost identical with his B1s except for slightly smaller driving wheels to improve their uphill work. These latter were popularly known as 'Imminghams', after the name bestowed on the first; the LNER classified them B4. In the same year Robinson turned out a small-wheeled, fast goods variant of the B4, which became LNER Class B9.

All these first Robinson 4-6-0 designs were outside two-cylinder, with separate splashers to each driving wheel and a clear-cut family resemblance. Suddenly and inexplicably, in 1912 Robinson switched to six inside-cylinder 4-6-0s for express work. These were the handsome big-boilered 'Sir Sam Fay' class (LNER B2 until 1945, then B19), named after cities served by the

Left: Ex-GC Robinson Atlantic, Class C4 No 5363, heads a Marylebone-Manchester express past West Ruislip.

Below left: Ex-GC Robinson Class B4 4-6-0 No 6104 was shedded at Lincoln when this 1938 shot was taken of her working the York-Harwich section of the 'North Country Continental' boat train past Escrick./*E R Wethersett: Ian Allan Library*

Below: Ex-GER Class B12 4-6-0 No 8521 wheels a Liverpool Street express away from Cambridge past Trumpington. The ugly ACFI feed-water heater behind the chimney was a post-grouping addition; B12s so equipped were popularly known as 'Hikers'. The train's first vehicle is ex-NER, the remainder typical ex-GER corridor/*E R Wethersett: Ian Allan Library*

Above: Gresley's rebuild of Class B12: No 8567 of Class B12/3 hurries a 1935 Clacton express — including a vintage ex-GER six-wheeler, second vehicle — past Chadwell Heath./*E R Wethersett: Ian Allan Library*

Above right: Before Pacifics were plentiful — an early post-Grouping scene at Hadley Wood, with ex-GN Ivatt Class D1 4-4-0 No 3049 (at this date green, like the train engine) piloting large Ivatt Atlantic, Class C1 No 4442 (the GNR royal engine) on the 17.30 Kings Cross-Newcastle./*Real Photographs*

Right: A typical Manchester-Marylebone express of the early post-Grouping years, in the Pennines near Dunsford Bridge headed by Robinson ex-GC Class D11 4-4-0 No 5510 *Princess Mary* in green livery. The first coach is an ex-GN 12wheeler, the next three ex-GC, the last two post-grouping LNER./*Real Photographs*

GCR apart from the first, which honoured the railway's forceful General Manager. Again, Robinson quickly produced a companion, small-wheeled version with the same graceful single splasher, the 'Glenalmonds' (LNER B8) for mixed traffic.

Robinson was still not finished with 4-6-0 experimentation, but meanwhile in 1913 he produced an inside-cylinder 4-4-0 that experts generally rate his most successful express passenger engine — the 'Director' 4-4-0 (LNER D10 and D11). With the same firebox but a much shorter boiler than 'Sir Sam', the 'Director' displayed equal if not greater power, showing up the 4-6-0's inability to heat its elongated boiler to maximum effect; for that matter, the 4-6-0 did not even measure up fully to the Robinson Atlantic in performance up the GC banks. After the grouping and until Gresley B17 4-6-0s, V2 2-6-2s and Pacifics were drafted to the GC, the 'Director' was generally the preferred power for the Marylebone-East Midlands-Sheffield and Manchester expresses. It was also Gresley's immediate post-grouping choice to help cover a motive power shortage in Scotland; as well as sending north a number of GN engines, Gresley rushed out 24 more 'Improved Directors' (the D11, with side-window cab) for intermediate Scottish passenger services, deeming them superior to any of the NBR's own 4-4-0s, such as the 'Scotts' and 'Glens'.

Robinson's final shot at an express passenger 4-6-0 was the four-cylinder 'Lord Faringdon' of 1917 (LNER B3), which became a class of six by 1920. But yet again performance failed to match looks. The LNER gave the engines every chance, even stationing them at Kings Cross and Leeds Copley Hill from 1923 to 1927 to work the crack Pullmans and other London-Leeds expresses (though this was probably less of a reasoned management decision than a personal gesture by the former GC man whom the LNER had appointed Running Superintendent of its Southern

L N E R
5510

Area). But unless the B3s were deftly fired and driven they gobbled coal; the Ivatt Atlantic's superb boiler gave as much at far less cost to the fireman — and the fuel bill.

Two more efforts brought Robinson's 4-6-0 designs up to nine, no less. One was a two outside-cylinder mixed-traffic design of 1917 utilising the same boiler as a contemporary GC 2-8-0; only three were built (LNER B6), even though GC enginemen thought more of them than Robinson's previous mixed traffic 4-6-0s. Finally, in 1921, came a four-cylinder mixed traffic variant of the 'Lord Faringdon' (LNER B7), with a hunger for coal that bespoke their derivation and earned them the lifelong nickname of 'Black Pigs'. Nevertheless, after 1923 the LNER built more and the class eventually totalled 38.

The GC 4-6-0s saw World War II through and many came into BR hands, though none survived state ownership for long. The passenger classes were blessed with apple-green livery by the LNER, which did not keep them all on the GC Section. The 1923-7 spell of the B3s on the GN main line has already been mentioned (after that three went to Immingham and were still frequent Kings Cross visitors on excursions from Grimsby), and the B4s had a much longer GN stay. In 1925 the whole class was despatched to Ardsley and Leeds Copley Hill sheds in the West Riding. Their Yorkshire-based jobs included the Kings Cross expresses between Doncaster and Leeds, as Pacifics were then weight-restricted over the Calder Viaduct at Wakefield. From 1933 to 1935 three were at March, chiefly for GN/GE Joint line work to Doncaster and York, but on summer Saturdays they would sometimes turn up in the GE heartland at Norwich. The B6s, too, spent time in the West Riding in the late 1920s and early 1930s, getting a frequent whiff of East Coast ozone from Scarborough down to Skegness on summer excursions. The other classes were scarcely ever shedded outside ex-GC territory, but the B7s' freight rosters in particular familiarised them with most of the LNER main line network from Newcastle up to London. Wartime graft even found a B7 — and *Glenalmond* of the B8s — as far north as Edinburgh on two recorded occasions.

From the GER the LNER inherited one of the two most successful inside-cylinder 4-6-0 designs in British history (the LNWR 'Prince of Wales' was the other). This S. D. Holden product of 1912, the LNER B12, was the more outstanding achievement because of the severe limits of height, width and weight within which GER designers had to operate. So well tailored were they to their difficult GE environment, with its sharp gradients, curvature and physical restrictions on engine bulk that when, in 1928, still heavier express loads made strengthening of GE power urgent Gresley

Top left: One of the NER 4-4-0 types: Class D17 4-4-0 No 1923 heads a southbound stopping train out of York./*Real Photographs*

Centre left: One of the NBR 4-4-0 types: Class D34 No 9291 *Glen Quioch* near Inverkeithing with an Edinburgh-Fife Coast train in 1936./*Ian Allan Library*

Bottom left: Gresley's first 2-6-0 type, the two-cylinder Class K2s, were frequently express passenger power on the Norwich-Cambridge-Liverpool Street route in the 1930s: No 4688 heads an express southward from Cambridge past Trumpington./*Ian Allan Library*

Below: Three-cylinder Class K3 2-6-0s pass at New Southgate: No 126 on an up express, No 134 on a down fitted freight./*Ian Allan Library*

supplemented his new B17 three-cylinder 4-6-0s with 10 more B12s that were only slightly modified by comparison with the original series. And from 1932 onwards, as B12 boilers and cylinder blocks wore out, 54 of the class were thought worth rejuvenating with modified B17 boilers, new valve arrangements and roomier cabs to become Class B12/3. This rebuild was actually the brainchild of Edward Thompson, then Gresley's assistant; its success fortified a belief in tinkering with his forbears' work that he was to indulge repeatedly when he succeeded Gresley. With their copper-capped chimneys and generous external application of brass beading the B12s were a joyous sight in their original GER royal blue livery, but post-World War I impoverishment enforced a change to austere grey, which did not finally give place to LNER green until 1929.

Apart from a short post-grouping trial of two B12s at Copley Hill and Doncaster, and the posting of one to Gorton for through Ipswich-Manchester working on 'North Country Continental' until a B17 took over in 1929, the only significant migration of class members from GE territory in LNER times was the gradual concentration in Scotland of all the engines not reboilered as B12/3. They were exported primarily for GNoS Section duty north of Aberdeen, though during World War II some were shedded in Edinburgh and Glasgow. Begun in 1931, this process was eventually completed in 1946. Only two B12s had been scrapped by nationalisation.

The GER also passed on to the LNER one of the outstanding types in the wide range of 4-4-0 classes the new company inherited for its intermediate and stopping passenger services. This was Holden's 'Claud Hamilton' (LNER D15), introduced in 1900 and multiplied in a succession of fresh batches up to 1911, by when it had become the GER's principal passenger engine. Holden's successor, A. J. Hill, developed the breed with a bigger boiler into the so-called 'Super-Claud' (LNER D16), of which 10 were built new at the GER's Stratford works in 1923; thereafter many of the earlier D15s were rebuilt in the same mould. Another pre-eminent 4-4-0 design, the GC 'Director', has already been discussed.

Biggest contributor of 4-4-0s to the LNER was the NER, which handed over 186. Of the classes that were longest-lived in LNER ownership, the similar Wilson Worsdell designs of NER Classes M and Q (lumped together as D17 by the LNER) had been shunted off the East Coast main line to sheds like Hull Botanic Gardens, Bridlington, Selby, Scarborough and West Hartlepool as soon as the NER Atlantics came on the scene. In their prime they had been front-rank Newcastle-Edinburgh power — in fact, Class M No 1620 was a star of the 1895 Race to the North, reputed to have covered the 124½ miles from Newcastle to Edinburgh in 112min, well below the subsequent 'Coronation' streamliner booking of 120min for the distance. The final NER 4-4-0 design, Worsdell's R1 (LNER D21) of 1908, was the biggest British 4-4-0 at the time of its debut; that made it a rather clumsy machine for secondary line use as bigger engines took over the main lines, with the result that much of the D21s' final years were spent as main-line pilots, especially in World War II.

The outstanding and most durable NER 4-4-0 was Worsdell's R of 1899 (LNER D20), the type which for years prior to the Atlantics' emergence monopolised 'the British Empire's Fastest Train', the Newcastle-Sheffield express booked over the 44.1 miles from Darlington to York in 43min. During the Atlantic period pairs of D20s were still deployed on East Coast expresses; later, and until Gresley produced his D49 4-4-0s, they were preferred power for the more significant NE Area secondary passenger services, such as Leeds to Hull and Scarborough or Newcastle to Car-

Left: A Robinson ex-GC Class Q4 0-8-0 under a characteristic LNER coaling plant: loaded coal wagons were lifted bodily up the flank to the top of the structure and then tippled to unload their contents into a massive overhead bunker./*Ian Allan Library*

Right: Raven ex-NER three-cylinder Class Q7 0-8-0 No 624 at York shed in 1929./*P Ransome-Wallis*

lisle, as well as main-line semi-fasts; most survived well into BR days for light work from sheds like Bridlington, Selby, West Hartlepool and Alnmouth.

Of the remaining 4-4-0 types, space constraints allow honourable mention only of W. P. Reid's series of simple, free-steaming and resilient inside-cylinder 4-4-0s for the North British: the mixed traffic, 6ft driving wheel 'Intermediates' of 1906-7 (LNER D32), conceived chiefly for the NBR's Aberdeen and Mallaig fish trains, which established the characteristics of Reid's subsequent 4-4-0s; the 6ft 6in 'Scotts' introduced in 1909 (LNER D29 and D30) for express passenger work and their 6ft mixed traffic derivatives (LNER D33); and Reid's updated 'Intermediate', the 6ft 'Glens' of 1913-20, which in particular withstood hammering over the fierce grades of the sinuous West Highland line from Glasgow to Fort William and Mallaig as well as, if not better than the more modern engines sent to the line in the 1930s — so much so that 'Glens' were still ranging the West Highland in early BR days.

Many of the mixed traffic designs offered to the LNER, it will be seen, were derived from express passenger types. Additionally, several companies fitted their bigger-wheeled goods 0-6-0s with continuous brake so that they could be appropriated for excursions or slow passenger trains in the peak periods. Most of the 4-6-0 types rendered the LNER yeoman mixed traffic service, especially the ex-GC B7s and a class so far unmentioned, Raven's 5ft 8in driving wheel, three-cylinder NER design of 1919 that became LNER Class B16. Gresley allowed more B16s to be built after the grouping and both he and Thompson thought the type worth updating in the light of subsequent steam locomotive practice. Though never based outside NER territory, the versatile, lusty-voiced B16s ranged most LNER main lines south of Edinburgh in their time, and that for most of them lasted into the 1960s. Before World War II the B16s made light of heavy express work where Pacifics were then prohibited — for instance, on Hull-Kings Cross expresses between the port and Doncaster — and tackled some massive merchandise freights in Yorkshire.

The mixed traffic type which Gresley adopted as the new LNER standard, however, was his own GN 2-6-0. The GWR was the first to demonstrate the mixed traffic virtues of this arrangement and Gresley, who had earlier pursued development of Ivatt's 0-6-0 range for combined operations, followed with his first 2-6-0 essay in 1912. That was under-boilered, a defect which was remedied in the two-cylinder K2 of 1914. Then, in 1920, Gresley turned out the first of the LNER's most numerous 2-6-0s, the chubby K3s with a 6ft diameter boiler, 5ft 8in driving wheels and three cylinders; this was the first class to embody the final form of Gresley's controversial conjugated motion, whereby

ROSE SMITH
N E
L N E R
6173

the inside, middle valve was operated by a motion derived from the outside valve gear. The K3s became a staple feature of practically every LNER main-line freight landscape and were also invaluable reserves for peak-period passenger work, on which they were more than once timed at 70mph-plus. The K2s were not so ubiquitous, but could be discovered in areas as remote from each other as the GE lines and the West Highland; some of the latter's K2s, incidentally, were graced with the names of Scottish lochs.

Three of the pre-1923 companies had 2-8-0s or 0-8-0s — or both — to offer for heavy freight haulage, and each one had an outstanding candidate or family of candidates — the GNR its Gresley 2-8-0s, the GCR its Robinson 2-8-0s and the NER the 0-8-0s of Worsdell and Raven. Together they satisfied LNER needs in this department right through to nationalisation, except for post-grouping additions to the stud of Gresley 2-8-0s and Edward Thompson's metamorphosis of some ex-GC O4s into his own O1 design.

Gresley began with a two-cylinder 2-8-0 (LNER O3) in late 1913. Though its debut was promptly followed by a lift of the standard Peterborough-London loaded coal train consist to 80 wagons, the O3 was heavy on coal, a failing attributed to its (for the time) oversized two cylinders. The O3s, incidentally, were the first really noisy performers of that characteristic Gresley outside-cylinder music — the rhythmic clank as pin play allowed coupling rods to strike wheel centres — for which railwaymen soon dubbed them 'Tangos'. Any defects in the O3 were rectified in Gresley's three-cylinder 2-8-0 (LNER O2), of which the prototype emerged from Doncaster in 1918. It was the wide measure of satisfaction with the O2 that resolved Gresley to adopt a three-cylinder arrangement in all his future designs.

Robinson of the GC had begun with an outside-cylinder 0-8-0 (LNER Q4) in 1902 and pre-dated Gresley with his 2-8-0 (LNER O4), which surfaced in 1911. This simple two-cylinder engine was probably the toughest workhorse ever created by a British locomotive engineer; however hamhandedly it was driven, however crudely it was maintained, however cruelly it was loaded, it never seemed to wince. Adopted as a War Department engine in both World Wars, it was called up for overseas service in several theatres, and saw service on home railways ranging from London South Western to Caledonian as well as its own territory when the World War I veterans of the class were demobbed to civilian owners. In later NER years the type was diversified into eight different parts as Gresley and Thomson prolonged the life of the O4s' rugged frames and running gear by mounting other boilers on them. Eventually, as already mentioned, Thompson was to create his standard LNER Class O1 two-cylinder 2-8-0 by rebuilding an O4.

The NER's eight-coupled engines were exclusively 0-8-0s. Worsdell began the line with his outside two-cylinder design of 1901 (Q5). His successor Raven produced a similar but superheated type (LNER Q6) in 1913, then his burly three-cylinder class of 1919 (Q7) — all sound, hard-working engines that met NE Area heavy freight needs throughout LNER days. Some of the NER's heavy industrial hauls were so short-distance that tank engines could cover them, hence Raven's small-wheeled three-cylinder 4-6-2 mineral tanks of 1910. The GCR, too, built 20 small-wheeled inside-cylinder 2-6-4Ts (LNER L3) in 1914-17 for coal haulage between Nottinghamshire pits and Immingham and Grimsby docks.

The GN, GC and NER all had eight-coupled tanks on goods work. The GN engines became freight engines by default. From his earlier 0-8-0 freight tender engines Ivatt evolved in 1903 an 0-8-2 to give — he hoped — the Kings Cross suburban trains more punch up the grades of London's Northern Heights. But the Metropolitan Railway baulked at accepting these ungainly machines over the Widened Lines into Moorgate and they were also uncomfortable at the speed demanded by some of the limited-stop peak-hour services. So they were demoted to coal train haulage between the Nottinghamshire coalfield yard at Colwick and New England yard, Peterborough, though in 1919 some did come back to Kings Cross for empty stock work until they were scrapped in the mid-1930s. The other two eight-coupled tank types, the NER's 4-8-0Ts by Worsdell and the GC's three 0-8-4Ts by Robinson, were specifically designed for marshalling yard hump work.

Over 2,500 tender 0-6-0s were passed to the LNER in 1923, representing more than a third of its total locomotive stock and more than one half its tender locomotives. Both they and the big fleet of 0-6-0 shunting tanks were of such variety that there is no room here to survey them adequately. Worth brief comment, though, are Hill's final 1920 GE design (LNER J20) with B12 4-6-0 boilers which overall were Britain's biggest 0-6-0s; Worsdell's last 0-6-0 designs of 1905-6 (LNER J26 and J27), whose 5ft 6in diameter boilers were the fattest of any British 0-6-0 in 1923; and

Top left: Ex-GN Class J6 0-6-0 No 3602 leaving Cambridge with a Hitchin branch freight in 1932./*E R Wethersett: Ian Allan Library*

Centre left: One of the massive ex-GER Class J20 0-6-0s, No 8275, heads up the Cambridge main line with a haul of coal from Whitemoor yard to London in 1935./*E R Wethersett: Ian Allan Library*

Bottom left: Robinson ex-GC Class S1 0-8-4T No 6173, working at Whitemoor yard in 1938; Robinson built three of these and Gresley two more as late as 1932./*P Ransome-Wallis*

Robinson's 1911 design (LNER J11), which 30 years after its birth Edward Thompson wanted to perpetuate as a post-World War II LNER standard type, and which were such nippy engines that they were often pressed into emergency use on Manchester-Liverpool fast trains via the CLC route in the mid-1930s. From 1926 to 1940, incidentally, a number of ex-NER J27s were sent to work from Cambridge, March and Peterborough East sheds on the GE Section; several J11s, too, saw East Anglian service from 1927 to the early 1930s, operating from Norwich, Lowestoft, Yarmouth and Cambridge.

Nor is there room to highlight more than the most proficient of the passenger tank classes that the LNER inherited. In the south, the most significant were the GE and GN 0-6-2Ts and the GC 4-6-2Ts, which are discussed in a subsequent chapter on the LNER's London suburban services. Up north, at the lower end of the size scale one must single out Wilson Worsdell's 0-4-4T built in substantial numbers between 1894 and 1901 (LNER G5), and of which over 100 were still doing manful service when BR took over in 1948. Smooth-running engines with a sprightly turn of speed, they not only bore the brunt of Newcastle and Leeds suburban services, but also took care of some longer-distance semi-fast workings, such as trains making the 49¾mile coastal run from Newcastle through Sunderland and West Hartlepool to Middlesbrough, until the emergence in 1913 of Raven's elegant 4-4-4Ts tended to concentrate the smaller engines on rural branches.

The three-cylinder Raven 4-4-4Ts, built to this unusual wheel arrangement with the aim of equalising riding quality in both chimney- and bunker-first directions, were deficient only in adhesion weight for starting and climbing; when Gresley rebuilt them as 4-6-2Ts in LNER days they became thoroughly sound engines. Finally one must record Scotland's dependence on Reid's doughty inside-cylinder 4-4-2Ts (LNER C15 and C16), built between 1911 and 1921, for the busy suburban services of Edinburgh and Glasgow until Gresley's V1 and V3 2-6-2Ts took shape.

Below: One of Raven's ex-NER Class H1 4-4-4Ts which were rebuilt by Gresley from 1931 as Class A8 4-6-2Ts; No 1326 heads a southbound stopping train out of York./*Real Photographs*

Right: Ex-NER Class G5 0-4-4T No 1912 moves a Leeds-Wetherby stopping train out of Collingham./*Real Photographs*

Below right: Light branch power: ex-GER Class F7 2-4-2T No 8307 on an auto-train at Quainton Road, Bucks. These stumpy little 4ft 10in-wheel engines were nicknamed the 'Crystal Palaces' by virtue of their big-windowed cab dwarfing the boiler./*Real Photographs*

1912

Gresley, Thompson and Peppercorn

As the LNER's Chief Mechanical Engineer, Nigel Gresley entered into a kingdom of twelve workshops. The GNR's Doncaster, the GER's Stratford, the H&BR's Hull Springhead, the NBR's Glasgow, Cowlairs and the GNoSR's Inverurie works had built both locomotives, coaches and wagons for their owners. The GCR has built its locomotives at Gorton, its coaches and wagons at Dunkinfield, both plants in the Manchester area. Best endowed of all was the NER, with locomotive works at Darlington and Gateshead, coach works at York and wagon works at Shildon. Under the LNER, locomotive construction was concentrated on Doncaster, Darlington and to a lesser extent Gorton, but all design work was ultimately concentrated on Doncaster. Springhead was closed in 1924, so was the M&GN's small works at Melton Constable, which had been mainly used to overhaul M&GN locomotives, though it had still undertaken a little new construction after M&GN motive power affairs passed into Midland Railway hands. The other inherited locomotive works were relegated to maintenance and repair work only.

At the start, as we have seen in the previous chapter, Gresley let construction of several pre-grouping types continue, from GC and NE 4-6-0s to GE and NB 0-6-2Ts — even some NER 0-4-0Ts. His immediate problem lay in Scotland, where a lot of ex-NB engines were dated or decrepit, and their replacement had been made more urgent by the NBR directorate's wily cessation of new construction as soon as Grouping had been politically agreed in 1921, so as to conserve their own cash. In 1924-5 Gresley had to switch north of the Border a number of 'foreign' engines — 10 GC O4 2-8-0s, 25 GC J9 0-6-0s, 14 GN K2 2-6-0s, 15 GN D1 4-4-0s and 12 NE J24 0-6-0s as a short-term palliative; in addition, as we have already seen, he had a new batch of GC 'Director' 4-4-0s built for the Scottish Area. Another GC type to gain Gresley's blessing was Robinson's A5 4-6-2T; in 1925 he ordered a new build of this design rather than the local product to cover a NE Area requirement for additional power on the key NE Coast short-distance services.

In 1925 Gresley's Pacific *Flying Scotsman* was displayed alongside the GWR 4-6-0 *Caerphilly Castle* at Wembley's British Empire Exhibition. On the basis of the arithmetical tractive effort formula, GWR propaganda claimed their 225lb boiler-pressure, four-cylinder 'Castle' to be more powerful than Gresley's heavier and bigger machine, with its 180lb pressure and three cylinders. And to Gresley's irritation, members of the GWR and LNER management arranged without his knowledge to put the issue to practical test on the track — whether with competitive intent or as a genuine offer to pool knowhow is still unclear. Whatever the motive, the outcome profoundly affected LNER design, for Gresley was always prepared to embody others' successful technology in his own practice.

The resulting trials of Gresley's No. 4474 *Victor Wild* on the GWR 'Cornish Riviera Express' and of the GWR *Pendennis Castle* on Kings Cross-Leeds expresses as far as Doncaster have been narrated in countless books. Enough to say here that on any objective assessment the 'Castle' outpointed the Pacific on almost every count, from coal consumption to timekeeping. Gresley reacted slowly, but eventually, from 1926 onwards, he applied Swindon principles to a succession of experiments with four Pacifics — *Gay Crusader, Centenary, Lemberg* and *Enterprise*. By 1927 he had finalised the improved A3 version of his original A1 type (or A10, as it was reclassified in the final LNER days). In 1928-9 Doncaster built the first batch of A3s from scratch, Nos. 2743-52, and in time all the original Gresley Pacifics were rebuilt to the same specification.

The principal changes in the A3 by comparison with the A1 were an increased boiler pressure of 220lb/sq in, enlarged superheating surface, reduction of cylinder diameter and redesigned valve gear with long lap. The higher boiler pressure and added superheating enhanced the tractive effort, giving the engines more punch at starting; and the modified valves allowed the Pacifics to be worked at the short cut-offs obviously so effective on the GW engines — in other words, at speed a driver could 'cut off' the supply of steam to the cylinders much earlier in the stroke, letting the steam do more of its work by expansion and thus economising in coal. These changes brought Pacific coal consumption on a 500train

Above right: Inside the erecting shop of Doncaster works, with an A3 and A4 Pacific in the foreground./*British Rail*

Right: Class A3 4-6-2 No 2747 *Coronach* climbing past New Southgate with the 16.00 Kings Cross-Leeds and Bradford in June, 1932. This was one of the two A3s subjected to smoke deflection experiments in the 1930s—in this case by cutting away the upper part of the smokebox door./*E R Wethersett: Ian Allan Library*

No 2747

No
99

between Kings Cross and Doncaster tumbling down from 50 to 38lb a mile.

Gresley's most massive engine was unveiled in 1925. The heavy Yorkshire coal traffic from the ex-GC Wath yard, near Barnsley, to Lancashire began its trans-Pennine haul up the daunting Worsborough bank to Penistone, 7 miles long and as steep as 1 in 40 in places. Up this hill a 1000ton train needed the rear-end help of two eight-coupled engines — and generally two in front as well — so Gresley had Beyer Peacock build one of their patent Beyer-Garratt articulated engines to cope with the banking job single-handed.

The resultant 2-8-8-2, No 2395, was a 178ton, six-cylinder mammoth with the characteristic short and massively fat Garratt boiler low-slung between its two wheeled units. With a nominal tractive effort twice that of a GC 2-8-0, which made it statistically Britain's most powerful steam locomotive, it amply fulfilled the specification. Operating practice was to start a maximum-load train of 63 wagons from Wath with a pair of 2-8-0s in front, then at Wombwell, with the steepest 1 in 40 pitch looming up, switch one to the rear and buffer up the Garratt behind it. The 2½miles of savage pounding from there to the top of the bank at West Silkstone Junction, then a coast back to the bottom, repeated about 20 times a day, was all No 2395 saw of the world until the bank was electrified as part of the Manchester-Sheffield 1.5kV dc scheme after nationalisation, whereafter No. 2395 — now remumbered 69999 — was exiled to bank Bristol-Birmingham main-line trains up the 1 in 37¾ Lickey Incline.

Another 1925 product was Gresley's two Pacific-boilered Class P1 freight 2-8-2s for the Peterborough-London coal traffic, to which there is extended reference in Chapter Seven. As mentioned there, Gresley applied to these 2-8-2s an American device which had taken his fancy, the booster — a dimunitive two-cylinder engine driving the small-wheeled trailing axle and powered from the main boiler, which could be cut in in the low-speed ranges to enhance tractive effort at starting and on steep banks. He had first experimented with this auxiliary on Ivatt Atlantic No. 4419 in 1923 and was later to try it on two ex-NE Atlantics, but in these applications the idea tended to

Left: The Worsborough banker, Class U1 Beyer-Garratt 2-8-8-2 No 2395, photographed after 1946 LNER renumbering as No 9999/*E R Wethersett: Ian Allan Library*

Below left: Wartime pressure: Class J39 0-6-0 No 2991 in express service on the Cambridge-Liverpool Street line in 1945./*E R Wethersett: Ian Allan Library*

Below: Class D49 4-4-0 No 264 *Stirlingshire* pounds upgrade near Inverkeithing with an Edinburgh-Perth train./*E R Wethersett: Ian Allan Library*

be self-defeating: it was an asset at starting, but once the train was rolling the boiler got breathless trying to supply both main and booster cylinders, so the boosters were eventually discarded. The only durable Gresley booster experiment was on Robinson's big Class S1 0-8-4Ts, used as hump shunters at the ex-GC Wath yard.

Gresley intended his next new design to be a lighter, smaller-wheeled version of his three-cylinder K3 2-6-0, but the LNER's mid-1920s concern for its cash position forced him to go for a less expensive inside-cylinder 0-6-0 design instead. The Darlington design office was told to draft a modernised version of the ex-NER J27 with bigger wheels, to widen its mixed traffic use. But Scottish clamour for modern power to deal with its Fifeshire coal traffic changed priorities. First of the new 0-6-0s to emerge, in 1926, was the 4ft 8in J38, a class which spent its entire life in Scotland. The 5ft 2in-wheel but otherwise similar J39 materialised later then same year; 289 of them were eventually built to make this the most numerous of all Gresley classes. The J39s were lusty machines, marred only by the excessive and costly axlebox wear to which any engine without a leading bogie is prone; they covered most of the system, with the notable exception of the southern end of the GN main line, and were entrusted with some semi-fast passenger work — on the GE

Above: In wartime black livery, one of the later, large-tender 'Football' series of Class B17, No 2854 *Sunderland,* heads the 17.49 Liverpool Street-Cambridge past Whittlesford in August, 1943./*E R Wethersett: Ian Allan Library*

Above right: Gresley's high-pressure water-tube boiler 'Hush-Hush' 4-6-4, No 10000, enters Kings Cross./*Ian Allan Library*

Southend line, for instance — as well as freight.

Still under pressure to economise, Gresley told his Darlington draughtsman to shape a 4-4-0 round the J39 boiler to satisfy a 1927 NE and Scottish Area need of new intermediate passenger engines. They came up with the three-cylinder D49, or 'Shires' as they were known through bearing the names of English and Scottish counties. Capable of impressive power output when pushed, the D49s were one of the Gresley products least cherished by enginemen, largely because of their churlish riding and appetite for coal. They seldom operated south of Doncaster, though the prototype No. 234 *Yorkshire* had a trip or two up the GC line to Marylebone in 1927 and the following year No. 245 *Lincolnshire* was briefly based at Kings Cross to sample the 'West Riding Pullman'. To reduce coal consumption, Gresley followed up experiments on two 'Shires' by fitting further batches of D49s with Lentz rotary cam poppet instead of piston

valves; built in 1932-5, these engines were named after hunts and popularly known as the 'Hunts'.

Generally unloved, too, was the three-cylinder Class B17, or 'Sandringham' 4-6-0 of 1928 — another hard, rough rider. Some of the B17s' failings could justifiably be debited to the size and weight limitations within which a more powerful engine for the GE main lines had to be contrived. They were essentially a North British Locomotive Co design; as his own staff were exceptionally busy at the time, Gresley handed over most of the drawing-board work as well as the building to the firm.

The first series of B17s, named after country houses, was concentrated in GE territory until the mid-1930s, except for one or two isolated in the Manchester area at Gorton, primarily for throughout working of the Harwich-Liverpool 'North Country Continental' between Ipswich and Manchester, and a trial allocation of three to the ex-GC London shed at Neasden in 1934-5. Thus the B17s had chalked up some GC main-line experience before, in 1936, a new batch with larger tenders was launched specifically for the ex-GC route.

Sporting the names and colours of Football League teams in LNER country, these later B17s were the 'Footballs'; and it was these engines, particularly those based at Leicester, which wrote the B17s' best performance into the record books. To the chagrin of the Great Western faith, for instance, Sheffield's No. 2863 *Everton* one 1937 day handsomely beat the 'Cheltenham Flyer's' start-to-pass timing of 18½ min from Swindon out to Steventon, 20.8miles, by a minute with the 215ton through train to York, bustling up to a peak of 88mph at Wantage Road. The GC-based B17s roamed further afield then the GE allocation; in the opposite direction, a Leicester 'Football' had a three-nights-a-week turn to Newcastle on the Marylebone - Stockton - West Hartlepool - Newcastle night train that was a 1937 innovation. Towards the end of the 1930s, however, A3 Pacifics and V2 2-6-2s were taking over the toughest GC line passenger jobs.

Gresley greeted the 1930s with a one-off monstrosity — the bloated-looking 4-6-4, bleakly painted in grey, that he had been conceiving since 1927 at Doncaster so secretively that it had been dubbed the 'Hush-Hush'. Its *raison d'être* was Gresley's conviction that a very high-pressure boiler feeding a two-stage compound system — two small inside cylinders to expand the steam at high pressure, then pass it on to two conventional outside, low pressure cylinders — would greatly improve effiency and reduce coal consumption. The guts of 4-6-4 No. 10000, which dictated its ungainly outline, was therefore a 450lb Yarrow water-tube boiler of marine type, comprising

an upper water drum conncected to two lower pairs of drums by serried ranks of arched tubes, round which the hot firebox gases circulated. No. 10000 successfully timed major East Coast main line expresses, but it was a prey to defects, especially leaking tubes; and besides incurring progressively heavier upkeep costs, the engine did not save coal to the degree expected. So in 1937, after it had lain cold for months, Gresley disappointedly had what some of his brother officers called the 'Galloping Sausage' rebuilt as an orthodox three-cylinder half-sister of his streamlined A4 Pacifics. Because of its size it was usually limited to Kings Cross-Doncaster duties. To the end it was Britain's one and only 4-6-4 tender engine.

Design of a new 2-6-2T had begun at Doncaster in late 1927, but it was pigeonholed after that year's catastrophic Sevenoaks derailment of a Southern 'River' 2-6-4T at speed had made railwaymen suspicious of tanks with single-axle leading bogies (and also of tanks for express passenger work, so that Gresley wrote off completely a contemporary 6ft 2in driving-wheel 2-6-2T design for the Liverpool Street-Southend line). The three-cylinder 2-6-2T, Class V1, eventually emerged in 1930 and the entire first batch went to Scotland, though one had Kings Cross area trials in 1931. The V1s and the very similar V3s, in fact, were all North Eastern and Scottish Area residents until a number were drafted to the Liverpool Street outer suburban services shortly before World War II.

The economic slump that depressed the 1930s inhibited Gresley from launching any new designs after the V1 until, in 1934, he sprang his second 2-8-2 design upon us, the magnificent P2. Express train loads over the difficult Edinburgh-Aberdeen load were climbing well beyond 400 tons, particularly on night services after the introduction of third-class sleeping cars, and beginning to out-run even Pacific capacity. The P2 was created specifically to work 550ton trains over this route without assistance.

Gresley had been profoundly impressed by the technology of André Chapelon, CME of the Paris-Orleans Railway. By a streamlining of all internal steam passages, with devices ranging from the use of poppet valves and rearrangement and enlargement of

Left: No 10000 after rebuilding as A4-style Class W1: a close-up of the electrically-lit motion.

Below left: Under the Thompson regime and to simplify maintenance in wartime all the streamliners had the valances above the driving wheels removed, among them Class W1 4-6-4 No 10000; it is emerging from Welwyn North Tunnel with an up express./*F R Hebron*

Below: Class V1 2-6-2T No 7664 (after LNER 1946 renumbering — previously No 420) at North Walsham on the 12.50 Cromer-Liverpool Street in May, 1948./*W A Camwell*

steam pipes to a twin blastpipe and double chimney, Chapelon had transformed one of his existing Pacifics' performance, achieving a thermal efficiency unprecedented in previous steam history. Many of Chapelon's proven theories were embodied in Gresley's three-cylinder, 6ft 2in driving-wheel P2, which had the biggest cylinder and firebox (except for the Garratt) of any Gresley engine.

On a demonstration run from Kings Cross in June, 1934 the prototype No 2001 *Cock o' the North* lifted a 20coach train of all but 650 tons up to Stoke summit at an average of close on 60mph without being severely extended. Indeed, if the P2s had been used on the heaviest East Coast main-line trains over long distances their career might have been wholly glorious. Their easy power north of Edinburgh was unquestioned, but their long, rigid wheelbase punished track on the route's curves, and the comparative shortness of their intineraries in Scotland made their coal consumption look extravagant in relation to revenue-earning mileage covered. In all there were six P2s. The second, No. 2001, was built to the same deflector-fronted shape as No. 2001, but with Walschaerts gear-driven piston instead of poppet valves; Nos. 2002-5, however, were given an A4-type, wedge-shaped front end and the first pair ware subsequently rebuilt in the same style.

Above: In original condition, Class P2 2-8-2 No 2001 *Cock o' the North* passes Inverkeithing with an Edinburgh-Aberdeen express in 1936./*E R Wethersett: Ian Allan Library*

Above right: One of the second batch of Class P2 2-8-2s, No 2005 *Thame of Fife,* heads an Edinburgh-Dundee semi-fast at Kirkcaldy in 1936./*E R Wethersett: Ian Allan Library*

Right: No 3649, one of the Class V2 2-6-2s built during World War II, in wartime black livery./*Cecil J Allen collection*

The streamlined A4 Pacific's debut dominated 1935. Its genesis as power for the 'Silver Jubilee' is described in Chapter Four. Underneath its shroud, the A4 followed basically the same three-cylinder layout as an A3, but with some important differences. Trials with an A3, *Lemberg,* had created a very fast runner by reduction of her cylinder diameter, so the A4's cylinders were similarly shrunk. A concomitant increase of the piston valve diameter eased the passage of steam between valves and cylinders. Special attention was paid to the smoothing and shaping of all steam passages, so that at high speed steam would flow freely on its rapid course from regulator to cylinders and then to exhaust. The cylinder change meant a loss of initial tractive effort compared with an A3, but this was more than offset by an increase of boiler pressure from 220 to 250lb.

Nº 2005

L N E R
3649

It is an ironic reflection on modern technology that nowadays weary months of road testing are insisted upon to get any bugs out of a new high-speed rail unit before it is allowed into public service whereas the first A4, *Silver Link,* was sent almost straight from the assembly line to work the 'Silver Jubilee' unaided for the train's inaugural fortnight — in other words, to run just over 4,500 miles at 70mph average. In fact, no lost time was booked against the prototype quartet of A4s, Nos. 2509-12, in their first 100,000 miles on the 'Jubilee'. Another outstanding record of endurance was credited to No. 4492 in 1937, when it headed the non-stop 'Flying Scotsman' for 44 consecutive days and on eight others made the Kings Cross-Edinburgh run with stops — 20,436 miles in 52 days, and all without trouble. Fittingly, the LNER directors had one of the later A4s and Gresley's 100th Pacifics, No. 4498, named after him — *Sir Nigel Gresley* as he had been dubbed in the 1936 Birthday Honours.

Four of the 1938 batch of A4s incorporated another French device to streamline steam flow — the Kylchap double blastpipe and double chimney, with which Gresley had first and briefly experimented on two D49s as early as 1928. The double-chimney engines were always better steamers, freer runners and more economical on coal, but strangely the single-chimney engines were never modified in the LNER's lifetime. Not until 1957-8, and then only after stubborn advocacy by Kings Cross depot in face of persistent bureaucratic rebuffs, were the whole class given Kylchap gear. The improvement was so marked that the A3s were similarly rebuilt and all the V2 2-6-2s might have been but for the imminent funeral of steam.

It was one of the first four Kylchap A4s, *Mallard*, that was picked for the world record run on July 3, 1938 (Gresley sensibly resisted advice that he choose No. 4498 *Sir Nigel Gresley*, then a single-chimney engine). Two years earlier the LMS had edgily stolen the British record with 114mph on the 'Coronation Scot's' pre-service press trip. *Mallard's* 1938 outing with three 'Coronation' twin-coach units and dynamometer car was mounted under the public cloak of brake trials, but the real objective was never in official question. Starting southbound from Barkston, just north of Grantham, *Mallard* was gunned on full regulator up to 74½mph on the climb to Stoke summit; within 6 miles down the other side she was up to 116mph, then for 2miles on end she held 120mph or over, reaching a peak of 126mph.

Some of the A4s' most spectacular feats were recorded during the war, when, dingily black-liveried, with running plate valances removed by Gresley's successor for easier maintenance and often sketchily maintained, they confronted huge loads. One April day in 1940 *Silver Link* backed down from Kings Cross shed to the terminus to pick up her train — but never got there; the 25coach, 850 ton cavalcade was so long that its leading coach protruded into Gasworks Tunnel. The A4 took time to lift this gargantuan load up the bank to Finsbury Park, but thereafter managed the 103miles to Grantham in 123min. And on another wartime occasion *Capercaillie* — one of the A4 sea-bird names later surrendered for that of an LNER director, in this case Sir *Charles Newton* — kept 700 tons moving steadily at 75mph on the level between Darlington and York.

The Gresley engine which in LNER legend 'won the war', however, was his three-cylinder, V2 2-6-2, Britain's most powerful mixed traffic engine until the advent of BR's 'Britannia' Pacific. Introduced in 1936, the prototype No. 4771 was named *Green Arrow* after an LNER express parcels scheme of the period. The V2s' weight barred them from nearly half the LNER system, but they gave versatile service on anything from slow and heavy freight to front-rank expresses on all the LNER trunk routes between London and Aberdeen; many ranked them the best all-round hauliers ever to work the difficult line between Edinburgh and Aberdeen. Their 6ft 2in driving wheels could and did twinkle up to 90mph-plus on East Coast main line expresses; at the other end of the passenger scale, it was a V2 that had to move the heaviest train Kings Cross has ever dispatched — a March, 1940 express of 26 coaches, loaded with 1,300 passengers and totting up to 850tons. Countless other V2 wartime assignments were not much less formidable.

Gresley's last two designs were the three-cylinder K4 2-6-0 of 1937, intended to eliminate piloting on the West Highland line, and the three-cylinder, lightweight V4 2-6-2 of 1941 for secondary line mixed traffic. Both were successful machines of great promise. Next, probably, would have been an imposing 4-8-2 to cope with the increasing weight of East Coast expresses, but suddenly Gresley succumbed to heart failure on April 5, 1941. His successor, who had worked resentfully in his shadow at Doncaster, dedicated himself to diminishing Gresley's legacy, not developing it.

To be fair to Edward Thompson, he took over in the bleakest circumstances. The war was going badly, skilled staff were getting scarcer, maintenance scantier, engineering materials ever harder to obtain and the pressure for economy stringent. But all that does

Top right: A Class V2 2-6-2 on GC main line express duty — shortly after the end of World War II No 4830, its green livery restored, approaches Saunderton with the 18.20 Marylebone-Bradford./*H K Harman*

Centre right: Three of Gresley's masterpieces lined up at Haymarket shed, Edinburgh — Class A3 4-6-2 No 2796 *Spearmint;* Class P2 2-8-2 No 2001 *Cock o' the North* and Class A4 4-6-2 No 2511 *Silver King.*/*Cecil J Allen collection*

Bottom right: How Gresley's 4-8-2 design of 1938 would have looked had World War II not put paid to its production./*From a painting by Jack Hill*

4830

2511
L N E R

L N E R

FLYING
SCOTSMAN
LNER
4482
No 4482

Nº

Nº
78

Preceding pages: The 'Flying Scotsman' in the late 1930s, headed by green-liveried class A4 4-6-2 No 4482 *Golden Eagle./From a painting by George Heiron*

Left: Two examples of the elderly secondary service types which Thompson needed to replace after World War II. Country stopping trains of the 1930s employed a motley collection of pre-1923 coaching stock, exemplified by this string of ex-GE six- and eight-wheelers on a Bishops Stortford-Cambridge all-stations service headed by ex-GE Class F3 2-4-2T No 8043./*Ian Allen Library*

Below left: The ex-GE Class E4 2-4-0s were the last British survivors of that wheel arrangement. In the late 1930s some migrated to the cross-Pennine line, where No 7478 is seen on a Penrith-Darlington service./*Eric Treacy*

Below: Class V4 2-6-2 No 3402./*British Rail*

Bottom: Post-nationalisation view of a Class B1 4-6-0: No 61026 *Ourebi* restarting a summer Saturday Manchester-Mablethorpe train out of Lincoln on July 25, 1959./*J Cupit*

not excuse Thompson's eagerness to expunge anything that savoured of Gresley influence, starting with some of Gresley's right-hand men at Doncaster. Apart from his paranoid characteristics, it was probably significant that Thompson, who had spent most of his career in the NER before becoming Mechanical Engineer at Doncaster in 1938, was married to the daughter of Sir Vincent Raven, to whom Gresley had been preferred as LNER CME.

The most pressing requirement on Thompson's agenda was a general-purpose engine to supersede his array of ageing pre-grouping secondary types. Gresley's response had been the V4, but Thompson immediately cancelled orders that had been placed for 10 more to follow the first two, Nos. 1701-2, and set to work on a two-cylinder 4-6-0, the B1. Experts are still at odds on whether the V4 would have been a stronger answer to the specification, performance-wise, but it would have been unarguably dearer to build. However,

Thompson Pacifics: (*Top*) the rebuilt No 4470 *Great Northern*, Class A1/1; (*Above*) Gresley 2-8-2 rebuilt as Class A2/2 No 2005 — in wartime black immediately after outshopping in 1943 and before name was replaced; (*Top right*) Class A2/1 No 3697, the adaptation of a V2, here seen as first paired with a V2 tender, which was later named *Duke of Rothesay*; (*Centre right*) Class A2/3 No 500 *Edward Thompson*; and (*Below right*) final form of Thompson's Class A2/3 Pacific with rimmed chimney — in BR days No 60511 *Airborne* leaves Newcastle Central with a Glasgow-Kings Cross Express./*E R Wethersett: Ian Allan Library; Eric Treacy*

another undoubted factor in the decision was Thompson's obsessive determination to discredit Gresley's three-cylinder, conjugate valve gear practice. One of his first self-appointed tasks as CME had been to circulate his directors with a catalogue of failures in traffic which in his view were attributable to the Gresley derived valve gear.

The 6ft 2in wheel B1 4-6-0s, sometimes known as 'Antelopes' by virtue of the wild deer names applied to

3697

EDWARD THOMPSON
L N E R
500
500

60511

61671
61671

L N E R
9002
9002

Above left: Thompson's two-cylinder 'Sandringham' rebuild: Class B2 4-6-0 No 61671 *Royal Sovereign,* which became the royal engine for London-Sandringham royal journeys, poses with the LNER Royal Train./*British Rail*

Left: Class L1 2-6-4T No 9002 on Liverpool Street suburban service duty; in front of the side tank is the Westinghouse pump, an essential on this duty because of the air-braking of ex-GE suburban stock./*P Ransome-Wallis*

Above: Thompson's standard 2-8-0 fashioned from ex-GC 2-8-0s: Class O1 No 6624./*E R Wethersett: Ian Allan Library*

the first few, were Thompson's only notable contribution to British locomotive practice. Introduced late in 1942, the B1 was economically constructed and had essentially the same boiler as the B17 and rebuilt B12 4-6-0s; in all 410 were built. With weight and dimensional characteristics that allowed them to roam the LNER almost at will, they yielded few if any points to the comparable LMS Class 5 or GW range of mixed traffic 4-6-0s.

Far more controversial were Thompson's big engine essays. Following the B1 he announced that he would build a 6ft 2in wheel Pacific to supersede everything from Gresley's P2s and V2s to his K3 2-6-0s and the pre-grouping mixed traffic 4-6-0s. To the anguish of Gresley's admirers, he produced his prototypes by mutilating the P2 2-8-2s beyond recognition, starting early in 1943 with No. 2005 *Thane of Fife*. The original boiler was retained, but shortened and marginally increased in pressure, and fronted by an overlong smokebox. This last was largely necessary because Thompson decided to retain three cylinders, but with individual Walschaerts gear to each cylinder and the drives divided between leading and middle axle; as he was also obliged to re-use as much of the original P2 parts as possible, including their short connecting rods, Thompson was forced to locate the bulky outside cylinders well back in a void between bogie and driving wheels. The outcome of this misshapen arrangement was frame weakness that induced all manner of other breakages and failures, as well as what one LNER engineer has described as 'terrifyingly' rough riding. Moreover, the reduction of adhesion weight by removal of a driving axle made the engines prone to slipping — a curse on the Scottish grades where the rebuilds were now restricted to the same loads as A3s. That meant they were no longer a match for the P2's original chores, so that the rebuilding had been an unnecessary, money-wasting failure. Unloved by anyone and all too often sidetracked for repair, these A2/2s ended as second rank engines at York and Peterborough and were the first ex-LNER Pacifics to be scrapped. The four A2/2s with V2 boiler which Thompson had built in 1944-5 to a similar arrangement instead of the last four of the final V2 batch were little better.

Most offensive of all Thompson works to Gresley men was his rebuilding of a Gresley Pacific: that it was a calculated move to depreciate his predecessor was obvious from his stubborn choice of the very first, *Great Northern*, as subject despite pleas from his colleagues to pick any one of the other 18 by then still un-rebuilt to A3. The essence of the operation was again to replace Gresley's conjugated gear with three independent Walschaerts motions and divided drive; and that once more predicated an ungainly layout of cylinders between bogie and driving wheels. But the revised engine, classified A1/1, showed no economy compared with an original Gresley Pacific and had the same propensity to slip on starting as Thompson's other Pacifics. With the additional discredit of unreliability, it finished its career as a semi-fast passenger and freight engine at Peterborough and Grantham.

Undeterred, Thompson pressed on with his 'standard' Pacific subsequently classified A2/3, which was basically a repeat of his 6ft 2in wheel P2 and V2 rebuilds, except for boiler pressure raised to 250lb. Although the 15 A2/3s were free runners and have many impressive high-speed performances credited to them, they suffered the general Thompson Pacific weaknesses, from bad riding to mechanical unreliability, and were substantially inferior to the later Peppercorn 4-6-2s.

During the war Thompson had drafted a motive power standardisation policy for the LNER and in 1945 it was published. There were to be just 10 standard classes, no fewer than seven of which were to be rebuilds of existing types. For express passenger traffic *Great Northern* was the prototype of an intended new A1 class, with the Thompson A2s in support for other heavy passsenger and freight work. For mixed traffic Thompson proposed his B1 4-6-0 and the 5ft 2in wheel two-cylinder K1 2-6-0 which he first demonstrated in early 1946 by re-shaping Gresley K4 No. 3445 with a B1 boiler and two cylinders; his successor had 70 K1s built new. For heavy freight the O1 2-8-0 was to be created by a nominal rebuild of the Robinson ex-GC O4 2-8-0 with B1 boiler, cylinder and valve gear, though the 58 O1s thus manufactured actually re-used little more than the main frames and wheel centres of the Robinson engines. The smaller freight engine was to be an updated ex-GC J11 0-6-0. To supersede all other ex-LNER passenger tank engines, Thompson designed the two-cylinder, 5ft 2in wheel L1 2-6-4T, with enough coal and water capacity for it to assume some tender engine duties. Unveiled in the spring of 1945, the L1s eventually totalled 100, but were unremarkable engines, tricky to steam well and extravagant to maintain. The Thompson stable was to be completed by the Q1 heavy shunting 0-8-0T,

Below: The final LNER look of the Gresley Pacific, with 'banjo' dome: Class A3 *Centenary,* renumbered 56 in Thompson's 1946 systematic recast of the previously haphazard LNER locomotive numbering, moves a midday Kings Cross express out of Leeds Central./*Eric Treacy*

Below right: Soon after nationalisation and still with original rimless chimney, Peppercorn Class A1 4-6-2 No 60117 *Bois Roussel* passes Holbeck with the up 'Yorkshire Pullman'./*Eric Treacy*

moulded out of ex-GC Q4 0-8-0 tender engines; an updated ex-GN J50 0-6-0T; and a light shunter.

Every other ex-LNER class was to be scrapped except for a few to be retained to the end of their useful life. These were: the A3 and A4 Pacifics; the B17 4-6-0s, but rebuilt with two cylinders as B2 (several were so treated); the D49 4-4-0s, possibly rebuilt (just one was profitlessly turned into an inside-cylinder 4-4-0 as a model); the B16 4-6-0s, with valve gear altered; the V1s, V2s and V3s unchanged; and the K3 2-6-0s rebuilt with two cylinders as K5 (one was thus modified). But with his retirement impending in mid-1946 Thompson can have entertained scant hope of executing his controversial plan.

His successor, Arthur Peppercorn, was a jovially uncomplicated man of skill and tact who quickly restored shaken morale at at Doncaster. Some Gresley men snubbed by Thompson were brought back into his team, for the objective was no longer to bury Gresley but to refine his achivements. Orders for more Thompson Pacifics were abruptly scrubbed and a new 6ft 2in three-cylinder, A2 scheduled that restored the traditional Doncaster line, even though the Peppercorn type maintained the three sets of Walschaerts gear and divided drive. Fifteen of them were built before nationalisation imposed a new all-line motive power policy.

From the A2 Peppercorn developed what many experts claim to have been Britain's most efficient Pacific, his three-cylinder, 6ft 8in A1, with three sets of Walschaerts gear, divided drive, bigger cylinders and firegrate area than the A4, and Kylchap double chimney and blastpipe as standard fitting (only four of his A2s had this last device). For several months streamlining, A4-style, was contemplated, but eventually rejected because it would have been complicated by the forward position of the inside cylinder. The first A1 emerged on the eve of nationalisation, but the new overlords allowed the balance of the order for 48 to be constructed.

No epoch-making feats are chalked up to the A1s and some drivers preferred A4s, not least because the A1s could be boisterous riders. The facts are, though, that the A1s during their lifetime amassed a better average daily mileage (216) than any other British locomotive type (25 per cent more than A4s in the 1950s, for instance): that they cost about a third less to maintain than a Stanier Pacific on the LMR, for example; and that the five A1s equipped with roller bearings throughout averaged 120,000 miles between overhauls — a 50per cent better record than the other Pacifics. Magnificently free-running engines that could match an A4 for load haulage and easily bustle up to three-figure speeds, the A1s, it has been justly claimed, were a fitting crown to 25 years of developing steam Pacific technology at Doncaster works.

Express Passenger Services

The new LNER management of 1923 was quick to put its mark on the system's chief train services. Recovery of pre-World War I standards had been sluggish and even by 1922 the principal East Coast trains were still 7 per cent slower than in 1914. But at a stroke the LNER chiefs chopped 40min off the 'Flying Scotsman's' Kings Cross-Edinburgh schedule in their first summer timetable of 1923, brought all the major West Riding cities 20-30min nearer London, restored the Great Central trains to very near their sprightly pre-war timings and re-introduced the 82min Liverpool Street-Parkeston Quay schedule of the Great Eastern's heavy Hook of Holland boat train.

The fast London-West Riding times were put up by the first of the LNER Pullman fleet, the 'Harrogate Pullman'. The LNER had Pullmans on its hands from the Great Eastern, whose American-born General Manager, Sir Henry Thornton, had misguidedly expected East Anglians to take to supplementary-fare travel. But the Pullmans prospered only on the Liverpool Street-Parkeston Quay boat trains. So, as the LNER inherited a GER-Pullman Car Co agreement with many years to run, it decided to switch most of the cars to the East Coast main line and run them as an integral train, instead of singly in ordinary expresses as the GER had done; two Pullmans remained in the Liverpool Street-Parkeston Quay 'Hook Continental formation' until 1939, however. The new Harrogate Pullman actually ran between Kings Cross and Newcastle, calling intermediately at Leeds,

Below: The short-lived 'Sheffield Pullman' of 1924, heading north past Knebworth behind Robinson ex-GC Class B2 4-6-0 No 425 *City of Liverpool;* the engine has the early 'L&NER' legend on the tender and had not yet been renumbered 5425 in the post-Grouping LNER scheme.

Pullmans on the GE line: (*Right*) a Newmarket race special, headed by ex-GE Class D16 4-4-0 No 8786 in original condition; and (*below right*) Pullmans — the sixth, seventh and eighth coaches — in the rake of the Liverpool Street-Harwich boat train, passing Bethnal Green behind Class B17 4-6-0 No 2822 *Alnwick Castle./Cecil J Allen collection*

L N E R
8786

2822

Harrogate and Ripon; between London and Leeds it restored the best pre-World War I transit time of 3hr 25min non-stop.

A second all-Pullman train was launched in the summer of 1924. Its first routings, though, were a failure. It started as a Sheffield Pullman, running non-stop to and from Nottingham Victoria via Grantham; journey time to Nottingham was 2hr 23min, to Sheffield 3hr 15min. At first the train left Kings Cross 10min ahead of the 'Harrogate Pullman' at 11.05 and returned from Sheffield at 16.45, but custom was poor and within a month the pattern was reversed to a Sheffield departure at 10.30 and a return from Kings Cross at 18.05. Nottingham remained indiffererent, so from April 1925 it was cut out of the itinerary. The Pullman now operated from Manchester Central, starting at 9.50, and ran non-stop from Sheffield Victoria via Retford to Kings Cross in 3min under 3hr for the 161¼ miles. But patronage was still discouraging and in the autumn of 1925 the Pullman service was completely revised, concentrating both trains on the West Riding complex and establishing a Pullman framework that persisted in essence for the rest of the LNER's life.

The Sheffield train was re-styled the 'West Riding Pullman', running at 11.10 from Kings Cross to Leeds and Bradford, which was served by reversing a portion of the train out of the then Leeds Central station to Bradford. The Leeds cars were worked empty to Harrogate, whence the up train started at 11.15. On its return, after attaching the up Bradford cars at Leeds, the 'West Riding Pullman' was away at 11.50 to reach Kings Cross at 15.15. Simultaneously with the 'West Riding Pullman' rearrangement the 11.20 'Harrogate Pullman' was pulled out of Leeds and sent via the Knottingley and Church Fenton route non-stop to Harrogate, 198¾miles in 3hr 43min, which was the country's longest daily non-stop working at the time. From Harrogate this Pullman was now extended to Edinburgh, where it was due at 19.35, as a consequence of which it was retitled the 'Edinburgh Pullman'.

The last major change came with construction of a new seven-car train of all-steel Pullmans in 1928. That spring the erstwhile 'Harrogate Pullman', now 'Edinburgh Pullman', was re-equipped with the new rake, once more routed into Leeds, extended beyond Edinburgh to Glasgow and yet again re-titled as the 'Queen of Scots'. At 11.15 from Kings Cross the 'Queen' gave Leeds a mid-morning service from London and, with a 10.05 return from Glasgow, an afternoon Pullman service back. To balance West Riding coverage, the 'West Riding Pullman' was switched to a 16.45 departure from Kings Cross. By now, incidentally, the Bradford cars were detached at Wakefield, worked via Batley to Bradford and then over one of the former GNR's remote extremities, the Queensbury branch, to Halifax.

In 1935 a Hull section, put on and off at Doncaster, was added to the West Riding train and it was renamed the 'Yorkshire Pullman' to emphasise its wider coverage of the county. To round off this Pullman's history — and run still further ahead of the general evolution of LNER express services — one should add that when the 'West Riding Limited' streamliner appeared in 1937 and bid for mid-morning business from Leeds, the Harrogate section was condensed to four cars and sent behind an ex-North Eastern Class D20 4-4-0 via York to Doncaster, there to link up with the Halifax-Bradford and Hull portions.

At the start of the new Pullman trains, as described earlier, some of the elegant ex-Great Central four-cylinder 'Lord Faringdon' 4-6-0s were drafted to the GN route to haul them, but the strangers were rather unreliable and gobbled coal. With the advent of the 'West Riding Pullman' the Ivatt Atlantics took a half-share of the service. The 4-4-2s soon displaced GC 4-6-0s completely and from 1926 into the early 1930s made the Pullmans their shop-window, except for a period in 1927-32 when ex-GC 'Director' 4-4-0s were applied to a share of the workings from the Leeds end. North of Harrogate ex-North Eastern Railway Raven Atlantics or Pacifics, or Gresley Pacifics, took charge of the Pullman, though for a brief period ex-North British Atlantics headed them between Edinburgh and Newcastle. The 'Directors' were displaced at Leeds almost as soon as the Southern Area's former GCR Running Superintendent had retired.

The zenith of Atlantic achievement on the Pullmans came in the early 1930s, when the 'Queen of Scots' was monopolised by a picked quartet of Leeds Copley Hill engines, each the treasure of a specific crew who kept it in sparkling trim both mechanically and visually, with its external pipework always beautifully polished. Exploits such as an average of 83.3mph throughout the 30.3miles from Stevenage to Huntingdon or Kings Cross to Leeds in 175min, despite two dead stands and three other severe signal checks, which were recorded with the 295ton Pullman train in this era would not embarrass a modern diesel.

One rake of Pullmans was retained on the GE line

Top right: Soon after its introduction, the 'Queen of Scots' on Crimple Viaduct near Harrogate, headed by Class A1 4-6-2 No 2579 *Dick Turpin*./*Ian Allan Library*

Gresley's celebrated quintuplet articulated restaurant-kitchen set for the London-Leeds service: (*Centre right*) posed with Ivatt Atlantic No 1456 after construction for the GNR; and (*Bottom right*) near the end of its life, at the head of a Leeds express leaving Kings Cross behind Peppercorn Class A2 4-6-2 No 525 *A H Peppercorn* in 1948./*E R Wethersett: Ian Allan Library*

1456
G N R
DINING SALOON

No 525
A
B
C
D

NO SMOKING

L N E R

Left: Early LNER coach furnishing: interior of a 1929 restaurant car./*Ian Allan Library*

Below left: The up 'Scarborough Flier' near Barkston in 1930, headed by Class A1 4-6-2 No 2553 *Prince of Wales./Cecil J Allen collection*

Right: View through the side passageway of an LNER corridor tender to the footplate.

after 1923, not for a regular weekday routine but for special services to the East Anglian coast. The first venture, a Sunday operation from Liverpool Street to Clacton and back under the title 'Clacton Belle', was so profitable that it prompted the LNER to use the train for a summer weekday programme from London to different resorts — Cromer, Sheringham, Yarmouth, Hunstanton, Skegness, etc — from day to day; on these outings, priced very competitively, the train ran as the 'Eastern Belle'. In its last, 1939 summer you could buy a week's seat on the 'Belle' and make successive day trips to five different resorts for just £1·32 third and £1·97½ first class! Another of its uses was for London-Newmarket race specials.

The only other regular Pullman operations on the LNER were in Scotland. In 1930 a Pullman restaurant car was inserted in some Glasgow-Edinburgh trains, to compete with similar facilities on the rival LMS route between the two cities. Between 1932 and 1936 further Pullman dining cars were deployed on the Edinburgh-Perth, Edinburgh-Dundee and Edinburgh-Carlisle routes; two of the four trains so adorned on the Edinburgh-Perth route were the down 'Night Scotsman' and up 'Highlandman' sleeping car expresses.

Expectedly the new LNER decided to adopt Gresley's distinctive bow-ended, elliptical-roof GNR main-line coach outline for the whole of the new system. It also standardised the GNR's varnished teak livery, applying it artificially to the coaches of the remaining constituent companies which had panelled their vehicles in other wood. That affronted one or two aesthetes, but they were a great deal more scandalised in later years when the LNER used the same finish for metal-bodied coaches. Another Gresley characteristic which the LNER inherited was his compound-bolster coach bogie, probably the smoothest riding of any devised by engineers of the pre-1948 railway companies.

A distinguishing feature of Gresley's coachwork for the GNR had been his use of articulation, mounting adjoining coach-ends on a single bogie to save weight. Initially he applied the device to suburban and stopping train coach-sets, but in 1919 came a pair of articulated tea-car twin-sets, each comprising a compartment composite and an open third with a pantry, for the Kings Cross-Leeds service. In the 1930s, incidentally, these twin-sets gravitated to York-Swindon operation on the historic Aberdeen-Penzance service; at 785 miles this was the longest through working in the country, though for most of its life no more than a single coach covered the whole itinerary.

Undoubtedly Gresley's most striking main-line essay in articulation was the quintuplet set he had built in 1921, consisting of two outer brake composites and first and third-class dining cars sandwiching a kitchen car in the centre, all carried on six bogies. Right up to World War II this unit was the hallmark of the 10.10 (10.15 in summer) Kings Cross-Leeds and its balancing afternoon train back. Another pioneering feature of the quintuplet was its use of electricity instead of gas for cooking, with batteries charged by dynamos belt-driven from the coach axles. Early in 1925 the LNER proclaimed that all its future coaching stock would be articulated, but this intention was not fulfilled.

Triplet kitchen-restaurant car sets figured in the first post-grouping main-line rakes ordered by the LNER, four complete trains for the Anglo-Scottish services, including the 'Flying Scotsman', which emerged in the autumn of 1924. Close on their tail came the first new Gresley stock for territory beyond the East Coast main line, an 11coach train for the Liverpool Street-Harwich 'Hook Continental' which entered service in April, 1925. This substantial train roused the GE line's inside-cylinder Holden 4-6-0s to epic work in maintaining its 82min schedule for the 68¾ slack-ridden and pretty severely graded miles from London to the Essex port. In the later 1930s, incidentally, Parkeston Quay's other main boat train, the 'North Country Continental' to and from Liverpool Central and Manchester Central (it conveyed York and Birmingham portions as well) also involved a remarkable 4-6-0 working, as it was hauled throughout between Ipswich and Manchester via March, Lincoln and Sheffield, 216 miles, by a Gresley three-cylinder Class B17 and an unchanged crew.

A new titled train inaugurated in the summer timetable of 1925 was to become one of the East Coast Route's speed showpieces. This was the 'Scarborough Flier', 11.50 from Kings Cross and non-stop to York, and 10.40 out of Scarborough in the opposite direction. By 1935, when it was also carrying through coaches to and from Whitby, its London-York time had been pared to a flat 3hr, necessitating a start-to-stop average speed of 62.9mph.

A recreudescence of the old East-West Anglo-Scottish rivalry sparked off spectacular development in 1928. In the midsummer of 1927 the LNER proudly proclaimed that the advance portion of the 'Flying Scotsman', the 9.50 from Kings Cross, would from July 11 run non-stop between Kings Cross and Newcastle for the first time. The LMS countered by erasing the Rugby, Crewe and Carlisle stops of the 'Royal Scot', as the 10.00 from Euston to Glasgow had just been named, and presenting a public image of non-stop running all the way from Euston to Glasgow and Edinburgh; however, the working timetable scheduled a pause at Carnforth, 236 miles from Euston, to change engines and another halt at Symington, north of Carlisle, to separate Glasgow and Edinburgh portions.

That autumn the LMS took delivery of its first 'Royal Scot' 4-6-0s. Now it could and did outdo the LNER, by switching the engine-changing rendezvous from Carnforth to Carlisle Kingmoor, 301 miles from Euston, and thus establishing a new British non-stop running mark.

The LNER riposted with a two-pronged attack. First it refurbished the 'Flying Scotsman' with a handsome pair of new train-sets, built to an expanded width of 9ft 3in. Externally the trains were cast in the familiar Gresley mould, but a distinguished interior designer, Sir Charles Allom, had been commissioned to create a new ambience within the coaches. His *tour de force* was the restaurant cars, which were integrally furnished in flossy Louis XIV style, with individual armchairs, concealed lighting behind translucent pelmets (luggage racks were discarded in favour of vestibule wardrobe cupboards) and hand-painted decor; one car was finished in soft blue and stone, the other in a pastel red and stone. The kitchen cars of the new trains were Britain's first with electric refrigerators. In the spring of 1929 the sets gained coaches rebuilt at Doncaster to incorporate a unisex hairdressing salon with adjoining waiting room and a ladies' retiring room, which was staffed by a woman attendant throughout the journey. Another unique member of the 'Scotsman's' crew was an itinerant newspaper and magazine vendor. The 'Scotsman' sets were further enhanced in 1930 by new first-class coaches with wide-windowed compartments styled like the restaurant cars and the extravagance of two-a-side seating in plushy armchairs. Finally, in 1932, the hairdressing salon-retiring room coaches were further rebuilt to include a neat cocktail bar.

These 'Flying Scotsman' flourishes were not the only LNER essays in new trainboard diversion. In 1930 the 10.10 Kings Cross-Leeds train-set had a

Above right: The restaurant car attendant hands out earphones to restaurant car passengers on the radio-equipped 10.10 Kings Cross-Leeds in the early 1930s.

Left: Cinema car converted from a bogie brake on the Leeds-Edinburgh service in 1936.

radio and record player fitted into one of its brakes and the rest of the train equipped with headphone sockets above the seats. The record player was switched on in tunnels, when radio reception was blotted out, to keep the programme continuous. The headphones available to passengers allowed them to adjust volume to taste. Passengers took to the idea and in 1932 the mid-day Kings Cross-Edinburgh train-sets were also blessed with radio, but the apparatus was withdrawn in 1935. Instead the LNER gave the 10.10 Kings Cross-Leeds and 15.15 back a spell with a cinema coach, converted from a full brake, which unfolded an hour-long programme of newsreels, cartoons and travelogues for a 5p admission charge; in its first year this Pathé cinema car pulled in over 35,000 patrons, so in 1936 another cinema coach was tried on the Leeds-Edinburgh run, but both had been abandoned before the outbreak of war. (One should add that there had been a one-day experiment in the showing of silent feature films on the 'Flying Scotsman' way back in March, 1924.)

But to revert to 1928. The second string to the LNER's bow that summer was *real* non-stop running throughout between Kings Cross and Edinburgh with the 'Flying Scotsman', by grace of Gresley's corridor tender. Through the latter's cramped, windowless side-passage the crew of the Class A3 Pacific then heading the express could change places at the halfway mark of the run with a relief which thus far had been 'riding the cushions' in the train — and, incidentally, enjoying a free meal in the dining car; what is more, footplate work on the non-stop was paid at double-time rates. The LNER took the non-stop decision rather late in the day and Doncaster had to hustle the building of the corridor tenders through the works within seven weeks of the issue of orders and drawings. In later years these tenders were taken over by streamlined A4 Pacifics.

The LMS cunningly stole the LNER thunder by secretly scheming still longer non-stop trips on Friday April 27, 1928, three days before curtain up, with a blare of publicity trumpets, on the non-stop 'Scotsman'. 'Royal Scot' 4-6-0 No 6113 *Cameronian* and compound 4-4-0 No 1054 had their tender capacities enlarged, the 'Royal Scot' train was split into separate Glasgow and Edinburgh portions, and the two engines

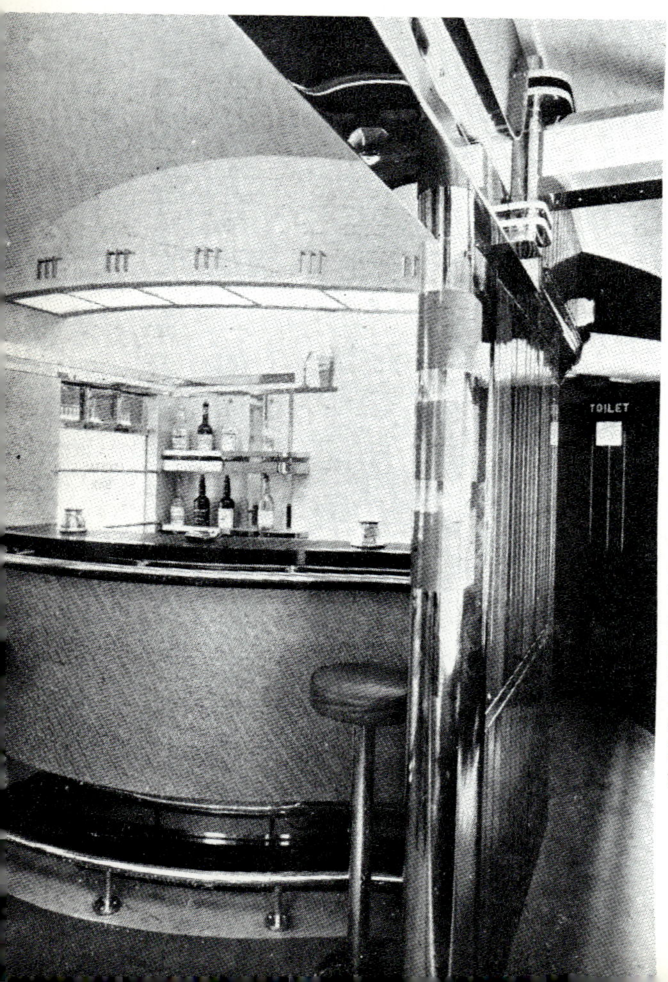

'Flying Scotsman' luxury in the 1930s: (*Above*) The first-class restaurant car in Louis XIV style; (*Left*) the cocktail bar introduced in 1932; (*Above right*) two-a-side seating — with loose cushions — in a first-class compartment of the 1938 train; (*Far top right*) the buffet car with side corridor in the new train-set of 1938; (*Right*) First-class saloon of the 1938 train-set.

respectively worked them to destination without any intermediate stop, covering 401½ and 399¾miles in the process. But it was a one-off stunt the LMS could not repeat day in, day out; and crowds still turned out the following Monday to applaud the departure of No 4472 *Flying Scotsman* from Kings Cross and No 2580 *Shotover* from Edinburgh on the first *regular* LNER non-stop runs, at 392¾miles the longest in the world's daily schedules at that time.

But the 'Scotsman' still had to spin out the same 8¼hr over the journey as it did when it was making four stops going down and five coming up. That meant a beggarly average of 47½mph, which was ludicrously slow compared with the pace to which other expresses were now timed. The rigidity of the 'Scotsman's' overall booking was the outcome of a pact not to compete by unilateral schedule-cutting that had been struck between the East and West Coast companies after the hectic 1888 and 1895 Races to the North. Conformity was still mandatory until 1932, when the LMS and LNER at last agreed that the minimum times set nearly 40 years earlier had become totally

ALARM SIGNAL

FLYING
SCOTSMAN
No. 4489
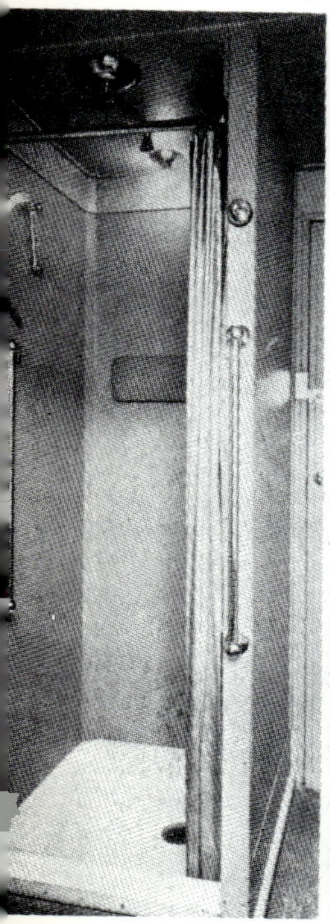

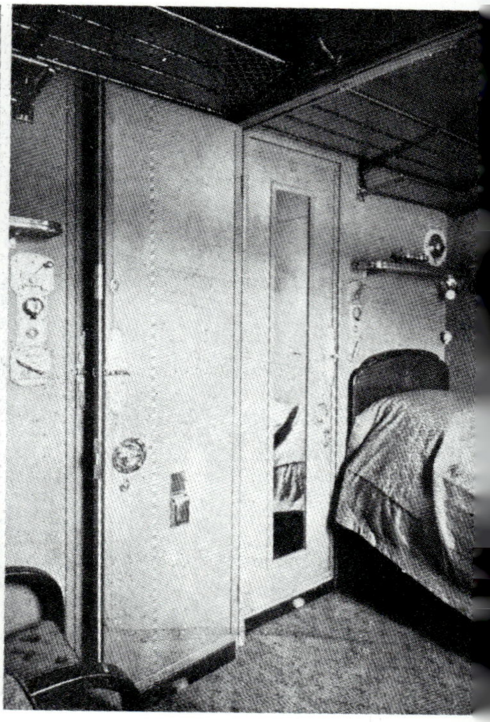

Above left: The down 'Flying Scotsman' immediately before World War II, passing Finsbury Park behind Class A4 4-6-2 No 4489 *Dominion of Canada,* wearing its presentation Canadian railroad bell./*Eric Treacy*

Left: Inside the prototype luxury sleeping car of 1932, showing (*left*) the shower-bath: and (*centre and right*) two adjoining compartments opened up to each other to form a suite.

Above: The 27 staff of the 'Northern Belle' cruise train pose with ex-NB Atlantic No 9876 *Waverley* at Aberdeen.

unrealistic each thereafter followed its own bent, provided the other was forewarned. So between 1932 — a year of general and substantial East Coast main line acceleration — and 1938 the 'Scotsman's' Kings Cross-Edinburgh transit time was progressively pared to 7hr non-stop and 7hr 20min with intermediate calls. By 1938 the train had again been re-equipped with heavy vehicles that could face the engine with a gross load of 600tons, passengers and luggage included, making it one of the most taxing haulage jobs on British rails. Non-stop running was confined to the summer service; in the winter it would have been difficult to drum up a trainload of passengers making the throughout London-Edinburgh journey. The main worry was to keep the non-stop Pacifics adequately supplied with water; the tenders' coal capacity was ample. Drivers of trains preceding the non-stop over certain troughs were ordered not to pick up water unless it was vital, to ensure that the 'Scotsman's' Pacific dipped its scoop into a brimming trough.

Other main lines meanwhile were not neglected. Also in 1932, for instance, the former GC express services from Marylebone to the East Midlands and Sheffield, battling for traffic with the Midland Division of the LMS, were re-stocked with new Gresley coaches and significantly accelerated. The key 7.30 up from Sheffield had its timing shorn of 33min at a stroke and the 16.45 back was revised to get its passengers into Sheffield by 20.02.

Nor was night travel ignored. In 1928 the LNER discarded the tradition that sleeping cars were for first-class passengers only. The initial third-class cars were convertible — that is, the compartments presented orthodox three-seats-a-side accommodation for day travel, but could be turned into four-berth bedrooms by adjusting the bench-seats and lowering hinged upper berths that folded into the wall. So the LNER at first was hedging its bets on the innovation, but its enterprise was quickly justified, even though the accommodation was pretty spartan by today's standards. In fact, it was the equivalent of a contemporary *couchette;* occupants were given only a pillow and a rug for their berth fee of 30p or 35p (according to dis-

tance) and the four berths per compartment had no individual lights. Nevertheless, demand was so quickly demonstrated that before 1928 was out Doncaster was ordered to build the first third-class cars for exclusive sleeping use, with fixed berths. Four years later the LNER went pioneering again with a couple of prototype first-class sleepers sporting electrically-heated shower-baths; in these cars, too, one centre compartment had an independent bed which, when removed, allowed the partition to be folded back so that two adjoining berths could be converted into a bedroom-lounge suite.

Another outstanding LNER enterprise was the 'Northern Belle' land-cruise, marketed four times in June of each year from 1933 to the outbreak of World War II. Operation had to be confined to that one month, because several of the train's 14 coaches were specialist vehicles sequestered from regular services: for example, the shower-bath sleepers just mentioned and the 'Scotsman's' hairdressing salon and cocktail bar could not be spared at the height of the summer. These and other 'gimmick' coaches, such as a full brake housing wardrobes for all on board, helped to make the 'Belle' a self-contained hotel. Royal trains alone excepted, it was undoubtedly the most lavishly staffed train ever run in Britain, with a crew of 27 to cater for the 60 passengers carried on each trip at an all-in fare of £20 (mid-1930s money terms!).

The 'Belle' did not always follow the same route. A specimen itinerary would run like this:

Friday night: departure from Kings Cross, dinner, bed and breakfast on the train.

Saturday: arrival at Harrogate for coach tour of the Yorkshire dales, then back on the train for a trip via Darlington over the Pennine line to Barnard Castle, where the 'Belle' was stabled for the night.

Above: Ex-GC Class B7 4-6-0 No 5466 on a train of 1933 green-and-cream 'Tourist' stock./*E R Wethersett: Ian Allan Library*

Right: Buffet car and saloon of 1933 Tourist stock./*Cecil J Allen collection*

Sunday: on by train from Barnard Castle over the Pennines to Penrith; the 'Belle' would be cut in two for this move, as no pair of engines allowable over the trans-Pennine line could have humped its 500tons-plus bulk up the fearsome gradients as one train. Then a second road coach tour, this time of Lakeland. Sunday night, on the move again by rail from Penrith via Carlisle and the Waverley route to Edinburgh.

Monday: sightseeing in the Scottish capital; Monday night, on to Aberdeen.

Tuesday: a Deeside coach tour; Tuesday night, back up the main line to Edinburgh's outskirts at Dalmeny for stabling.

Wednesday: a morning run to Balloch for a steamer trip up Loch Lomond, what time the train retreated to Dumbarton, shed its sleeping cars, and took the West Highland line. It would re-embark the passengers from the loch steamer at Ardlui, then ferry them on to Fort William and Mallaig. The sleeping cars having been worked separately down the West Highland line, Wednesday night's dinner and bed would be taken in the train.

Thursday: back up the West Highland line — with the train again split into day and night sections because of the fierce gradients — to Arrochar & Tarbet. Here the passengers would be decanted on to a

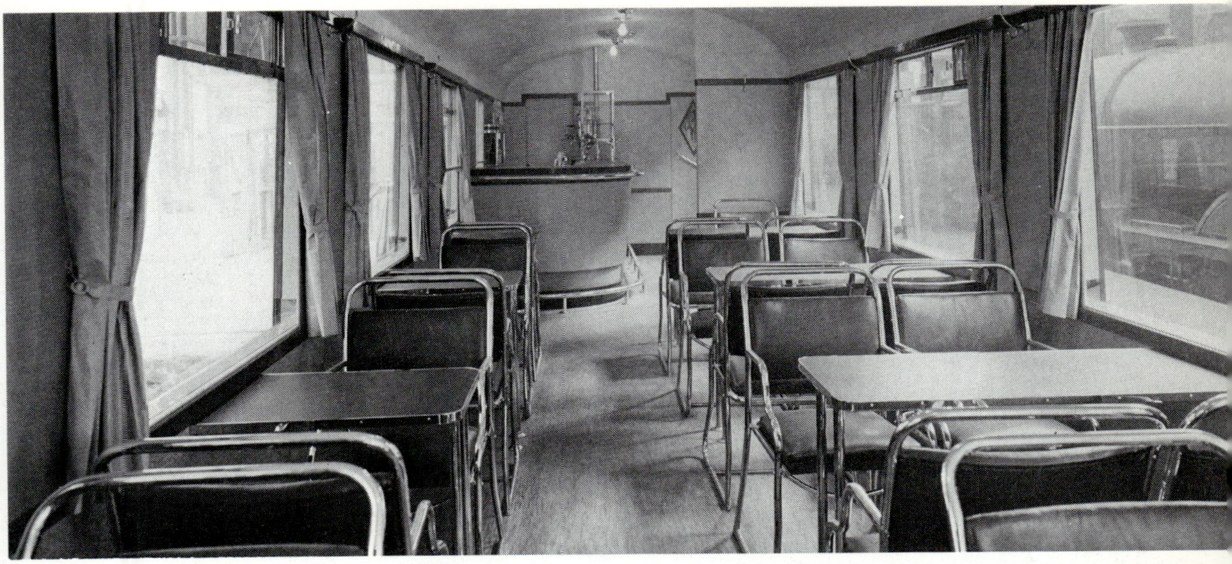

LNER
Nº 4441

NE
1
1
1531

Clyde steamer at the head of Loch Long for a cruise through the Kyles of Bute and up-river to Craigendoran, there to be re-united with the 'Belle' at teatime; then, with the 'Belle' once more re-assembled as one train, on to Edinburgh for a last spree in the Scottish capital before a late-night departure to Kings Cross.

Friday: Cruise finale in the London terminal at 11.00.

By the mid-1930s road transport was starting to sap the railways' holiday and excursion business. As a countermove the LNER launched in 1933 its 'Tourist' train-sets. These were 12coach units, all third class in open salons with high-capacity bucket seating at tables. Each set comprised two brake-ends, two buffet cars and four articulated twin-sets.

For carnival effect they were painted rather garishly cream above the waistline and apple green below, a garb that got shabby the more quickly because the rising cost of teak had induced an experiment with plywood panelling that weathered badly. It was soon replaced by steel, which from then on was increasingly used instead of wood, until in Edward Thompson's era at Doncaster steel panelling was standardised for all new LNER coaching stock.

At the other extreme of the passenger comfort scale, Gresley took a step in the direction of air-conditioning in 1934. To the train-set of the businessmen's 17.30 Kings Cross-Newcastle (a year later its path was to be taken over by the 'Silver Jubilee' streamliner) he fitted pressure ventilation. This was the forerunner of air-conditioning proper, which requires thorough insulation of the coach interior. With pressure ventilation conditioned air was injected into the compartments at floor level by an underframe-mounted, electrically-powered fan and steam heater under thermostatic control.

An entertaining new venture of 1932 was what the timetable soberly listed as 'Garden Cities and Cambridge Buffet Expresses', but what Cambridge colleges more pithily branded the 'Beer Trains'. The winding, freight-heavy exit from Liverpool Street had always inhibited a fast service of Cambridge by the GE Line, so the LNER decided to develop the easier though slightly longer route from Kings Cross and the branch from Hitchin. At first the five trains each way were just three coaches long; one was a buffet car — hence the 'Beer Train' alias — and in the others the third-class setting was only three-a-side, a luxury in those days. The 'Garden Cities' in the official name were Letchworth and Welwyn Garden City, at which, with Hitchin and later Royston in some cases, the trains called intermediately.

The service made an instantaneous impact. Soon loads were six and occasionally up to ten coaches, what time schedules were screwed up to 75min down and 72min up for the 58½ miles between Kings Cross and Cambridge, stops included. The ex-GE 'Claud' and ex-GN Ivatt 4-4-0s or 'Klondyke' 4-4-2s that initiated the service had to yield to the large Ivatt 4-4-2s, which revelled in an Indian summer, chirruping lustily up to the Northern Heights summit at Potters Bar as they had with longer-distance expresses in pre-Pacific days.

In the succeeding years to World War II the LNER developed the regular buffet-car express theme on other shorter-distance routes that were being plundered by road competition. The 'Beer Train' buffet cars had been improvised from existing open thirds, but from 1933 new, purpose-built all-electric cars were built. To reinforce their sales-appeal, the LNER fixed the tariffs in these buffet cars at levels well below those of full restaurant cars.

The Newcastle-Carlisle and Hull-Liverpool services acquired new buffet cars in 1935. Next, in 1937 the GE Line operators decided that they had exaggerated the speed handicaps on their Cambridge line and put on a thrice-daily service of five-car buffet expresses which knitted Liverpool Street to Cambridge in an unprecedented 65min running time for the 55¾miles; omission of a Bishops Stortford stop by these trains was exceptional, too. And in the same year new six-car corridor rakes with buffet car transformed the North-East Coast-Newcastle-Sunderland-Stockton-Middlesbrough interval service, until then always covered by non-corridor stock. Other buffet car rakes were introduced between Leeds and Scarborough.

After years of yielding schedule best between the Forth-Clyde Valley and Aberdeen to the ex-Caledonian and later LMS route from Glasgow, the LNER now had the tools to excel on the ex-NB line from Edinburgh. To a growing stud of Pacifics and Class V2 2-6-2s had been added Gresley's massive Class P2 2-8-2s, conceived with the Scottish East Coast Route's sharp gradients and need for power for acceleration from inconvenient speed restrictions particularly in mind. At last, in 1937, the LNER could maintain 3hr overall timings between Edinburgh and Aberdeen; that put the Granite City within 10¼hr of London by connection off the down 'Flying Scotsman' and cut the time distance to 9¾hr southbound, by a feed out of the 12.45 from Aberdeen at Edinburgh into the up 'Coronation' streamliner off the 12.45 from Aberdeen.

By then, of course, we were well into the LNER streamliner era. But that deserves a chapter to itself.

Above left: A 'Beer Train' — Class C1 4-4-2 No 4441 speeds past Knebworth with a Cambridge-Kings Cross buffet car express./*E R Wethersett: Ian Allan Library*

Left: The final shape of LNER express coaching stock: the Thompson design of 1945, with entrance doors and lateral vestibules 'amidships'./*British Rail*

The Streamliners

The 1930s were the decade that transformed the image of the express passenger train. In the autumn of 1932 Britain boasted the world's fastest daily train in the LWR 'Cheltenham Flyer' with its 71.4mph average, 65min booking for the 77.3miles from Swindon to Paddington. By the outbreak of World War II, though, Britain's quickest was well below the hundredth mark in the world league table, beaten out of sight by the capacity for sustained high speed of new diesel traction in the United States and Germany.

Europeans were awakened to diesel potential in May, 1933, when the Germans put into daily service the first of the streamlined diesel multiple-units that was to interlace all the country's key cities at high speed by the outbreak of war. This flagship of a subsequent fleet was the 'Fliegende Hamburger'. At a stroke it lifted the world mark for fastest everyday working to 77.4mph, covering the 178 miles from Berlin to Hamburg in 138min and regularly touching 100mph en route.

Now that the LNER was free of the crippling 1895 agreement it had inherited to peg Anglo-Scottish overall journey times, as mentioned in the previous chapter, it was eager to push East Coast main-line speed to the practical limit. The new German diesel flyer looked the tool for the job and Gresley was bidden to seek estimates from Germany for the cost and likely London-Newcastle performance of a three-car-unit. The Germans responded with data that put a ceiling of 4¼hr on feasible Kings Cross-Newcastle timings. The LNER management felt a Gresley Pacific

Below: The up 'Silver Jubilee' slows for the Peterborough North curve, with Class A4 4-6-2 No 2511 *Silver King's* chime whistle wailing. Engine and train are in the original silver-and-grey livery. In the train's early months No 2511 was the Gateshead reserve engine and rarely worked the 'Jubilee'./*Cecil J Allen collection*

Below right: Simultaneous departure from Newcastle Central in May 1936 of the up 'Silver Jubilee', headed by Class A4 4-6-2 No 2509 *Silver Link,* and the 10.00 Newcastle-Liverpool, powered by Gresley Class A1 4-6-2 No 2582 *Sir Hugo.*/ *Cecil J Allen collection*

could do better; furthermore, they suspected Tyneside and Teesside businessmen would sniff at the more cramped seating and cold buffet service of the diesel unit compared to the growing comfort and full kitchen fare of conventional East Route expresses.

Before accepting the challenge, Gresley prudently put one of his existing Pacifics to the test. On November 30, 1934, No 4472 *Flying Scotsman*, no less, was hitched to a four-car train and handed over to a flamboyant driver of the day, Bill Sparshatt, for a spin to Leeds. He spurred the Pacific out of the local station at Kings Cross so fiercely that it nearly took to the ballast before Gasworks Tunnel. They were through Peterborough in a few seconds under the even hour — unimaginable in those days — and No 4472 went on to eat up the last 3 miles of 1 in 178 to Stoke summit at a then unheard of 81 mph. Grantham, 105½miles, was passed in 83½min and the special rolled into Leeds, 185¾miles, in just under 2hr 32min from London.

It had all been so easy that two coaches were added for the return trip, totting the six-coach load up to 205 tons. Unconcerned, No 4472 made it back to Kings Cross in 2hr 37min; the time would have been less had not Sparshatt's fireman ended up understandably feeling the strain of 371½miles' work, 250 of them at 80mph average. But he and Sparshatt had made a mark in rail history, for coming up No 4472 had hit the first fully authenticated 100mph on British rails during the descent of Stoke bank. (The GWR 4-4-0 *City of Truro's* claimed 102mph in 1904 is open to question.)

Early the following year the LNER management decided to pin its faith to steam and in March, 1935 Doncaster was ordered to build new train-sets and four new Pacifics, the latter to the design on which Gresley and his staff had been developing since the previous spring from their Class P2 2-8-2. Before finalising his new Pacific concept Gresley elected for one more high-speed test of an existing Pacific. This time he chose an A3, No 2750 *Papyrus*, whereas at the time of its 1934 exploit No 4472 had been the earlier-pattern A1 and had not undergone the cylinder and valve modifications Gresley adopted after the 1925 Exchange, or had its boiler pressure and superheating increased.

The date was March 5, 1935, the course this time Kings Cross to Newcastle, and the load six coaches. Despite a dead stand for several seconds and some ultra-slow running near Doncaster because of a freight derailment, *Papyrus* made Newcastle in three minutes under 4hr, ridiculing the German diesel men's assessment of 4¼hr as par for the 268.3miles. After a mere 2¾hr break for servicing *Papyrus* returned to Kings Cross, now with Sparshatt in charge; for this test, remembering how the fireman had inevitably wilted

towards the end of the 1934 Leeds double journey, Gresley had organised a separate crew each way. For 12 miles down Stoke bank Sparshatt averaged 100mph, touching a new British steam peak of 108mph. Overall the the Newcastle-Kings Cross transit time was trimmed a bit more to just under 3hr 52min; and of the day's total 536¾miles' running, some 300 had been achieved at an average of 80mph.

The new train emerged in late September, 1935, named 'Silver Jubilee' in honour of the year's completion of 25 years' reign by King George V and Queen Mary and styled externally to reflect its title. The seven-coach set, comprising a brake first articulated twin with mixed open (at first two-a-side only, but later modified to three-a-side) and compartment (two-a-side) seating, a restaurant-kitchen articulated triplet, and a brake third open articulated twin, was clad in silver-grey rexine with sparkling stainless steel trim, topped by aluminium spray-painted roofs. Up front, the first of Gresley's new streamlined A4 Pacifics was liveried silver-grey to match. Laboratory tests had convinced Gresley that in the 70-100mph speed range the air resistance of a conventional express train doubled, until at 100mph it was sapping as much as 85 per cent of the power generated by the lcomotive. As well as streamlining the locomotive, therefore, he faired off the train as effectively as he could by closing the gaps between coach ends with rubber sheeting and dipping underframe panels between the bogies to within 10in of rail level.

'Silver Jubilee' journeys were to span mealtimes — 10.00 to 14.00 coming up and 17.30 to 21.30 going down — and the service was directed at business travel in particular, hence the high proportion of catering and first-class accommodation in the limited seven-car set. The exceptional speed and comfort, enhanced by pressure ventilation and double glazing to limit travel noise, justified supplementary fares, and it cost 25p first-class and 15p third-class to ride the train, even if you were on a railway pass or employee's privilage ticket. That was quite a stiff charge for the period, since lunch on the 'Jubilee', believe it or not, cost only 17½p and dinner 25p in first-class, 22½p in third-class seats.

Just three days before the public service launch of the 'Silver Jubilee' the LNER laid on a press demonstration run that is now legendary. The footplate crew of No. 2509 *Silver Link* had been told to put her on a loose rein so as to convince Fleet Street that the A4s had a reserve in hand even on a 4hr timing to Newcastle, but probably even Gresley himself was taken aback by what followed that Friday afternoon, September 27, 1935.

At 14.25 *Silver Link* forged easily out of London, accelerating the 220ton train up to a then unprecedented 75mph on the 1 in 200 climb to Potters Bar. Through Hatfield, where curve and pointwork set up the first of the sickening lurches that were to blench more and more faces in the train as the afternoon hectically unfolded, *Silver Link* was making 95mph. Woolmer Green summit brought her down only to 88mph, so that beyond the crest she was soon into 'the ton', storming through 107mph at Hitchin to a maximum of 112½mph at Sandy. For 25miles on end actual speed was in three figures and over 43 miles the average was 100mph. This high-speed belt was cut short so finely, with the then severely restricted Offord curves alongside the Ouse river only a mile away, that at least one LNER man on board was palely certain drowning was seconds ahead. The 76½miles from Kings Cross to Peterborough were torn off in 55min and the 105½miles to Grantham in just over 88min, but as Grantham came into sight *Silver Link* was catching signals from the conventional Leeds express that had left London 45min ahead of her.

Commercially, the 'Jubilee' — or 'Silver Bullet', as

A 'Coronation' train-set complete with beaver-tail observation car./*Cecil J Allen collection*

its regular clients soon dubbed it — was an instantaneous success. Advance booking was almost essential to be sure of a seat. The often boisterous riding of the train did not disconcert Tyneside businessmen, who were impassive to the waiters' nighty ritual of flower-vase removal from the dining car tables as the train climbed out of Kings Cross. The most stomach-wrenching roll would evoke only a grunted 'Lively tonight, isn't it?' from the regulars. By 1937, however, the ride had been softened somewhat by application of rubber blocks to the suspension, to dampen lateral movement, and re-equipment with longer-wheelbase articulated bogies. Third-class demand was such that in early 1938 an additional vehicle was built to make the third-class unit a triplet and the whole train eight coaches grossing 248 tons. Incidentally one novel facility introduced on the 'Jubilee' for a brief period in 1936 was a library service.

In the spring of 1936 planning of a second streamliner began. The first concept envisaged a London-Aberdeen service, stopping intermediately at Newcastle, Edinburgh, Kirkcaldy, Dundee and Montrose; Kings Cross departure would have been 12.15, Aberdeen arrival 21.15, and coming up the train would have been 9.15 out of Aberdeen, 18.15 into Kings Cross. Between Kings Cross and Newcastle timings would have been identical with the 'Jubilee's', save for omission of the latter's Darlington stop each way, so that the new streamliner was to be booked between Kings Cross and Newcastle in 3hr 55min non-stop each way. But a heavier train than the 'Jubilee' was in mind and so further measured tests of an A4's capacity were ordered, with a shot at a new maximum speed record on the side.

For the first and only time this deliberate attempt at a new British rail speed peak was made with a load of fare-paying passengers. It was conducted with the up 'Jubilee' on August 27, 1936; the engine was No 2512 *Silver Fox*, with dynamometer car inserted between it and train. Knowing what was planned, I had gone to Kings Cross to meet the 'Jubilee' that afternoon. When 14.00 went by without its appearance, one couldn't restrain some morbid worry. Then, at nearly seven minutes past, a rhythmic crescendo of jetting steam pierced the general hubbub of the terminus, suddenly exploding fortissimo as *Silver Fox* limped out of Gasworks Tunnel with steam spurting out under its bufferbeam. When she had staggered to a stop one heard that a new record had been notched up on Stoke bank, but only just, at 113mph, and at a price. The engine had been driven with less finesse than in earlier demonstrations: she had been so hammered

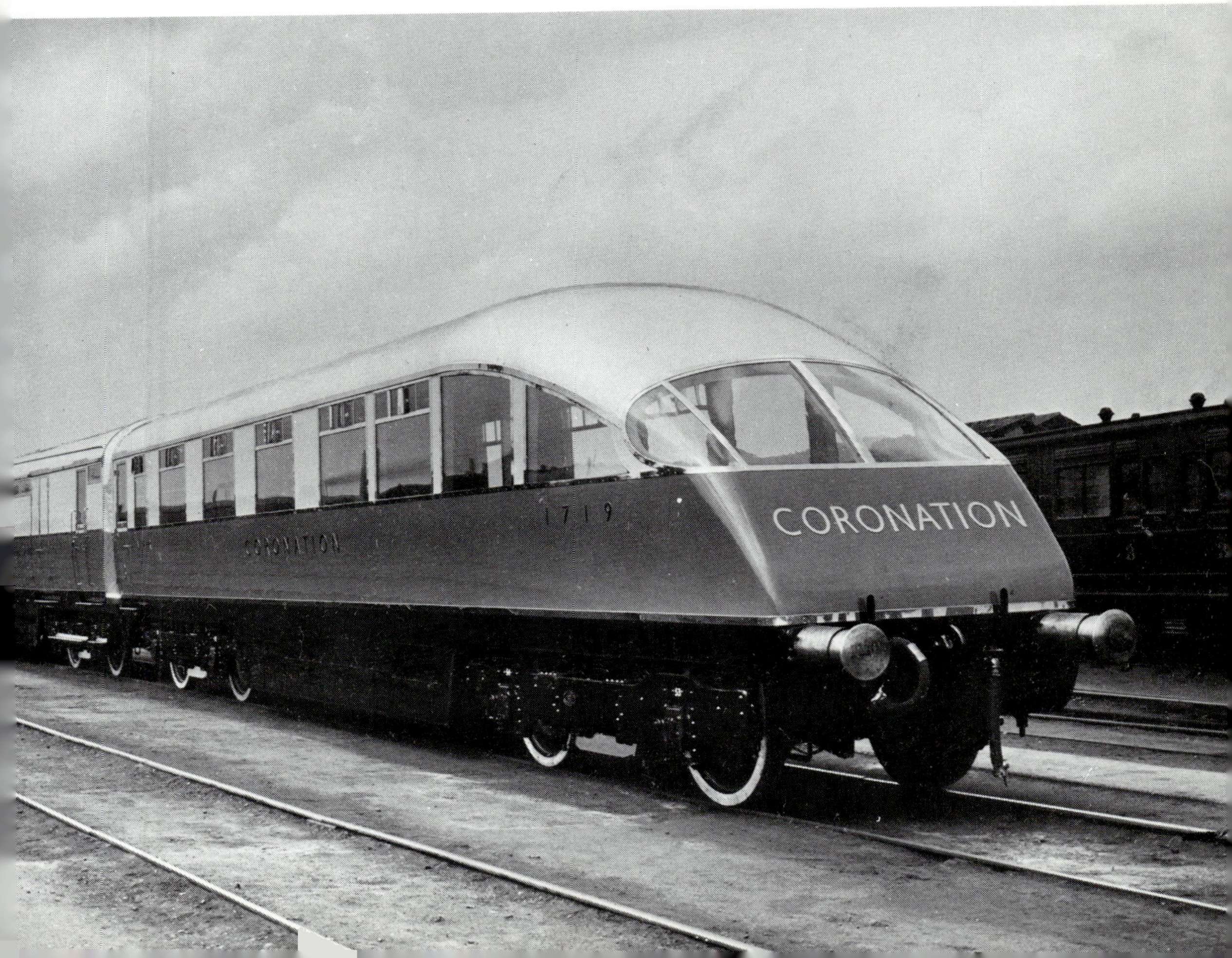

that the big-end bearing metal of the middle cylinder had overheated to melting point, allowing the big-end itself so much play that it had knocked out the cylinder end.

For the return working with 'Jubilee' and dynamometer car that night Sparshatt turned out with *Silver Link* to give a display of skill that proved an A4 could cope comfortably with a 10coach load on the streamliner schedule. And on September 26, a Newcastle-Edinburgh test with No 2511 *Silver King* satisfied the LNER that a 2hr allowance for this northern stretch was perfectly practicable; that was 30min faster than the 'Flying Scotsman's' schedule at the time.

In the event the LNER decided to restrict the Anglo-Scottish streamliner's itinerary to London-Edinburgh. Named 'Coronation', the new flyer made its debut on July 3, 1937, after a press demonstration on June 30 that misfired slightly. Two days earlier the LMS had nervily grabbed the record by edging its new 'Coronation Scot' up to 114mph so close to Crewe that the train all but left the track as it curved into the station. The driver of No 4489 *Dominion of Canada* was told to regain the crown on Stoke Bank, but he could only manage 109½mph.

The 'Coronation's' daily schedule did earn the LNER a title, however, for its 157min timing over the 188.2miles from Kings Cross to a York stop represented a 71.9mph average, a British start-to-stop record. Leaving Kings Cross at 16.00, it was into Edinburgh at 22.00 with York the only intermediate call. Coming up, the 'Coronation' was 16.30 out of Edinburgh and 22.30 into Kings Cross, in this direction with a call en route at Newcastle only. Later a Newcastle stop was added to the northbound schedule, but without addition to the overall time. With its nine-coach formation of 312tons when the observation car was added and its strenuous schedule south of York, the 'Coronation' handed the A4s by far their most demanding streamliner assignment, especially in winter. More than once firemen were scouring their tender floors for coal in the last few miles; on two known occasions, in fact, the up train had run right out of coal by Hitchen.

Externally the 'Coronation' train-sets followed the 'Jubilee' pattern, except that they were decked out in two-tone blue — above the waistline light Marlborough blue and below, dark Garter blue, in which a new batch of A4s were liveried to correspond. But internally the accommodation was open throughout, though with each first-class bay and every pair of third-class bays enclosed by partitions to dispel customer antipathy to very long-distance travel in saloons. That allowed meals to be served at every seat; and thus each set included two kitchen cars in its four articulated twin-sets, the remaining cars being two brake thirds, two thirds and two firsts. Seating was arranged two-and-one with tables in the thirds, and in the firsts one-and-one in swivelling armchairs that could be turned in to cut-away tables for meals and afterwards rotated 45deg away from them to let the occupants freely stretch their legs. Both pressure ventilation systems and sound insulation were an improvement on the 'Jubilee'.

Ninth vehicle in a 'Coronation' set was the independent beaver-tail observation car, with its deep swivelling armchairs that cost 5p for an hour's occupation. This was detached in winter, when darkness deprived it of point and the valiant A4 up front was glad of any load relief. At the end of each journey, of course, the

Left: Interior of a 'Coronation' first-class saloon./*Cecil J Allen collection*

Above right: Interior of a 'Coronation' observation car./*Cecil J Allen collection*

Right: The 'Coronation' and a Leeds and Bradford express left Kings Cross simultaneously at 16.00. Between the Kings Cross tunnels No 4466 *Herring Gull* on the streamliner draws away from Class W1 4-6-4 No 10000 on the West Riding express, which ran slow line to Finsbury Park, then switched to the main line behind the 'Coronation'./*C C B Herbert*

Nº 4466

Nº 4492

A
C
D
Nº 2509

Above left: Class A4 4-6-2 No 4492 *Dominion of New Zealand* hustles the northbound 'Coronation' past Marshmoor, near Hatfield./*Ian Allan Library*

Left: By now repainted in garter blue, Class A4 4-6-2 No 2509 *Silver Link* starts the down 'West Riding Limited' out of Kings Cross./*Ian Allan Library*

Above: Class B17/6 4-6-0 No 2870 *City of London*, one of the pair of 'Sandringhams' streamlined to work the 'East Anglian' in the autumn of 1937.

observation car had to be turned as well as the locomotive.

In the autumn of 1937, on September 27, a third streamliner was launched. Blue-liveried like the 'Coronation' and with a similar formation of four articulated twins — but no observation car — the 'West Riding Limited' was 19.10 out of Kings Cross, 21.53 into Leeds and 22.15 into Bradford; coming up, it left Bradford at 11.10, Leeds at 11.31 and reached Kings Cross at 14.15. New A4s Nos 4496 *Golden Fleece* and *Golden Shuttle* were specially named to reflect the train's West Riding industrial connection. The Pacifics worked the train only between Kings Cross and Leeds; between Leeds and Bradford this streamliner was incongruously hitched to a pair of Class N1 0-6-2Ts.

At the outbreak of World War II all three streamliners were swept from the timetables, never to reappear. Some of the stock was destroyed during the war, but in 1948 two of the 'Jubilee' set's units were exhumed for the Scottish Region 'Fife Coast Express' and in the same year surviving 'Coronation' and 'West Riding Limited' units were brought out and distributed among East Coast express services. All are now scrapped, but the two 'Coronation' observation cars survive in private ownership, one in Scotland and the other in Yorkshire.

The 'East Anglian's' credentials for inclusion in this chapter, frankly, are largely that to work it two Class B17 4-6-0s, Nos 2859 *East Anglian* and 2870 *City of London*, were clothed in an A4-type streamlined casing purely for publicity value. The Liverpool Street-Norwich route, to which the train was introduced on September 27, 1937, was too weight-restricted and slack-infested to allow of startling speed or of big, new engines to achieve it. So the six-coach train-set was built to standard Gresely outline, with no pretensions to air-smoothing. Inside, however, decor and furnishing palely imitated streamliner style, with meal service to all seats, which were armchair in both classes but three-a-side in first- as well as third-class. Departure from Norwich was at 11.55, with return from Liverpool Street at 18.40, and journey time was 2¼hr each way. The service title was dropped at the onset of war, but in this case the coaches remained in anonymous GE line use and then, after overhaul, were re-introduced as the 'East Anglian' from October, 1946. The two B17s were disrobed of their streamlining in 1951.

The London Suburban Services

Liverpool Street is still London's busiest terminus. The Southern's Waterloo handles more trains in a day, but Liverpool Street has a bigger throughput of passengers, even though its business has steadily declined in the past 50 years. Back in 1923, the LNER took on at the GER's headquarters the world's most intensive steam suburban service.

It was an extraordinary operation that would not disgrace modern electric traction. In fact, the GER would have electrified if it had had the cash. At first that seemed the only way to lift the burden the GER had been heaping on its back since the mid-19th Century by eagerly stimulating North-East London dormitory development through cheap fares. As late as 1920 you could still get an early morning return from Enfield Town to Liverpool Street costing less than one present-day penny for 21½miles' travel, and have the option of several trains on which to use it; even by 1927 the LNER had raised this minimum fare only to 2½p in today's terms. Such tactics had increased the population of suburbs like Walthamstow and Edmonton eight- and nine-fold in the 30 years up to 1900 (to Walthamstow, incidentally, the GER ran the country's first all-night service, at half-hourly intervals, from 1897).

So it was that by 1920 the GER was passing nearly 230,000 passengers a day through Liverpool Street. In the two-hour morning or evening peak 67-68,000 passengers flooded into or out of the terminus in jam-packed, spartan trains. To run more and improve travelling conditions looked impossible without electric traction, for there was certainly no room to enlarge the six-track approaches to the station. But a very resourceful GER management eventually solved its problem by some ingenious track, signalling and timetable reorganisation that made room for over 50per cent more rush-hour trains — and all for 2½per cent of what electrification would have cost.

At the start of the 1920s pressure was most intense on the West Side of the Liverpool Street layout, where Cambridge line traffic and its branch trains to and from Enfield, Chingford and Palace Gates were handled. To platforms 1 to 4, which dealt with the suburban trains, the GER operators applied rigidly patterned working. At the same time they remodelled the layout at the platform throats, so that each road had its own independent engine bay; thus an incoming train engine could be released behind its departing coaches to its own bay, then back on to the head of the next train into that platform without encroaching on operations at any of the other platforms. Other alterations included signalling devices to allow trains to run at closer headways on the 1 in 70 bank up to Bethnal Green than the orthodox block signalling arrangements allowed.

Each of platforms 1 to 4 was now reserved to a specific service and its trains were received and dispatched at a fixed-interval sequence. Following each other at 2min intervals, a train would leave No 4 for Wood Street, then one from No 3 to Enfield, then one from No 2 to Chingford and finally one from No 1 to Enfield or Palace Gates; behind each one trailed the engine that had brought it in, shuffling quickly into its bay to await its next turn, what time it was topped up with coal and water as necessary. Now came a 4min period during which a matching group of arriving trains was platformed, then the whole sequence was repeated.

To accelerate the processing of the passengers themselves, the circulating area behind the platforms was enlarged, the trains were boldly placarded and branded with code numbers to indicate destination and pattern of stops, and the three classes of train accommodation were made easily identifiable by painting blue (first class) and yellow (second class) bands between coach windows and roofs. It was this last touch that inspired the popular nickname of 'Jazz Trains', whereas the GER labelled the operation more prosaically an 'Intensive Service'.

The outcome was a miraculous shoehorning of 24 trains per hour on to each of the two suburban lines approaching Liverpool Street's West Side in the peak period. Each train had an 848seat capacity, so that a single track would be moving over 20,000 passengers in the hour. In those early days commuters were herded into crude, gas-lit four-wheelers, 16 to a train, some

Top right: The peak of the Liverpool Street 'Jazz Train' intensive service — crowded tracks at the top of Bethnal Green bank./*Ian Allan Library*

Centre right: A typical GE Line local service train of ex-GER six-wheelers in the earliest LNER days: ex-GER Class F3 2-4-2T No 8075 leaves Colchester with a Walton-on-the-Naze train./*Real Photographs*

Bottom right: A Liverpool Street suburban train of 1938: Class N7 0-6-2T No 988 with a standard ex-GE eight-car set on a Shenfield working at Chadwell Heath./*E R Wethersett: Ian Allan Library*

8075

SHENFIELD

of which were later made a bit more tolerable by conversion into bogie vehicles through the welding of two bodies into one. Not until 1925 did the Liverpool Street suburban services start to acquire new Gresley 10-coach train-sets, each comprising a pair of articulated quintuplets, to work alongside ex-GE eight-car non-articulated sets.

At the start this phenomenal service was mainly powered by diminutive late 19th Century GER 0-6-0, 2-4-2 and 0-4-4 tanks. Hill's chunky Class N7 0-6-2Ts, the principal Liverpool Street suburban power of the later 1920s and 1930s, were not yet available in quantity and even by 1930 had not completely ousted the smaller engines. Whatever the steam power, though, to mount such an operation on lines that were clambering up an implacable 1 in 70 so soon after leaving the platform ends was a remarkably bold enterprise.

The Jazz Trains were worked at the same full stretch until the 1926 General Strike, during which the LNER had a breathing space to reapparise the market situation. By now suburbia was edging further out, industry was burgeoning on the rim of the city, especially in the Lea Valley, and commuter demand was easing in the inner suburbs. Thereafter the West Side timetable was thinned out somewhat.

But the same outer suburban development that was relaxing tension on the West Side was now hitting the East Side's suburban services hard. By the 1930s overcrowding between Ilford and Shenfield was desperate, and the quadrupling of the layout from Romford to Shenfield that the LNER was able with Government aid to complete in 1934 was only a palliative, not a cure. The public clamoured for electrification, which the LNER could not afford.

Then in 1935 the Government stepped in, as described in Chapter Seven. Within a defined London suburban area revenue was pooled as a basis for coordinated development of integrated rather than self-interested modernisation schemes, and Government-guaranteed loans were made available for

Left: Almost masked by one of the somersault-type semaphores that were the hallmark of GNR signalling, an LMS Class 3F 'Jinty' 0-6-0T heads a Broad Street-Gordon Hill train down the Hertford loop in the 1930s./*Cecil J Allen collection*

Right: Well into LNER days ex-GN flat-roofed stock was stlll prevalent on Kings Cross outer suburban services. Soon after the grouping a Class K2 2-6-0 still carrying its GN number, 1678, leaves the main station with several six-wheelers at the front of its semi-fast, while a Class N1 0-6-2T climbs away from the Moorgate line platform with a new Gresley articulated inner suburban set./*Real Photographs*

new projects. In all, over £42million was laid on the table, of which about half was budgeted for combined LNER-LPTB schemes. A relieved LNER withdrew a half-hearted plan of its own for an underground line from Liverpool Street to Ilford, which it had propounded as a despairing sop to public opinion in 1930. Instead there was to be an extension of the LPTB Central Line Tube into LNER territory, combined with 1.5kV dc electrification of the LNER main line from Liverpool Street to Shenfield; and as mentioned later, the LPTB Northern Line was to take over the ex-GN High Barnet and Edgware branches. Neither the Central Line extension nor the Shenfield electrification was completed before the outbreak of World War II.

Fenchurch Street station pre-dated Liverpool Street and was the City of London's first railway terminus. At the grouping it became LNER property, for in the mid-19th Century the Great Eastern had taken over the working of both the London & Blackwall Railway that originated the station and the London Tilbury & Southend trains that were subsequently added to its traffic. Until Liverpool Street's 1874 opening, in fact, Fenchurch Street was the GER's main London suburban station. In 1882 the LTSR gained complete independence, but in 1912 the Midland cunningly engineered its takeover, aiming for better access to London docks. By dint of very keen fare pricing and by timetabling at speeds that prodigiously exerted its 4-4-2 tanks with loads running up to 13 bogies, the LTS had induced rapid residential growth on Thames-side and enormously increased its commuter traffic. Its season ticketholders were now encouraged by Midland promises of electrification and GER undertakings to equip an enlarged Fenchurch Street to match. But World War I intervened and between the wars the schemes lapsed for lack of cash.

However, the continuing growth and intensification of the former LTS and, post-1923, LMS Thames-side services compelled the LNER in 1932-5 to rebuild the station layout and re-cast its signalling round a new 140-lever box. The LMS trains, operated at tight 4min intervals in the peak, now predominated the station's 370 movements daily and gathered in most of its 70 000 daily passengers, but LNER locals still shuffled in and out of the station until after World War II, connecting with the ex-GE lines at Bow. Indeed, the LNER's original Liverpool Street-Shenfield electrification plan of 1936 budgeted for a shuttle service between Fenchurch Street and a bay at Stratford, to connect across platform with the Shenfield trains one side and LT Central Tube trains the other; in due course the catenary was erected, but no regular service was ever operated since it was eventually decided this would have extravagantly duplicated existing LT facilities. As for the LNER's steam services, the Fenchurch Street-North Woolwich service was suspended in the October, 1940 blitz and never resumed; Fenchurch Street-Loughton workings ended with the arrival of Central Line Tube trains at Leytonstone in May, 1947; and in November, 1949 the surviving Ilford line services were abolished concurrently with the start of the Liverpool Street-Shenfield electric working.

Most engaging of all London suburban services over LNER metals — except to their users — were the rush-hour trains between the old North London terminus of Broad Street, Liverpool Street's higher-level neighbour, and the GN Northern Heights suburbs of High Barnet, Alexandra Palace, New Barnet, Potters Bar and Gordon Hill. Until the mid-1930s the LMS was still content to rattle the bones of the wretched Broad Street commuter in sets of vintage North London Railway gas-lit four-wheelers, the third-class coaches of which harked well back into the 19th Century with their penitentially hard wooden seats and compartments devoid of partition walls above the luggage racks. The old North London outside-cylinder 4-4-0 tanks yielded in the 1930s to 'Jinty' 0-6-0Ts and these — apart from brief trials of a Fowler 2-6-2T — were still all the LMS saw fit to provide when the four-wheelers were at last replaced by LMS bogie stock. A

L N E R
4760

L N E R
5024

highlight of any weeknight's lineside show in the North London outskirts in the 1930s was the spectacle of a 'Jinty' scuttling non-stop from Finsbury Park to New Barnet on the 'Stockbrokers Special', the 5.7pm Broad Street-Potters Bar; that was always an entertaining curtain-raiser to the main drama of the down 'Silver Jubilee' storming northwards a few minutes later. In February 1940 the LNER took over the trains, but the following October German bombs put Broad Street out of commission for several days and the services to the LNER suburbs were not resumed until the war was over.

Kings Cross suburban travellers, both inner and outer, also had to contend with a good deal of ex-GN non-bogie coaches in the early days of the LNER, but in the mid-1920s Gresley began re-equipment of both services with articulated stock: twin-units for the outer suburban trains and eight-car sets of two quadruplets apiece for the inner suburban trains. Not that the latter were a startling advance in comfort on the GN stock. True, all seats were upholstered, but their narrow compartments and shallow, straight-backed seating well deserved the 'Sit-up-and-beg' nickname they acquired; and sometimes the bouncy suspension of the articulation made for a sick-making ride.

Until the debut of the Thompson Class B1 4-6-0 just before nationalisation, ex-GN types — 4-4-0s and both small- and large-boilered 4-4-2s — predominated on the outer suburban trains, apart from ex-GE Class D16 4-4-0s and Class B12 4-6-0s, and later Class B17 4-6-0s, that Cambridge shed would send out on its Kings Cross turns. These Cambridge representatives included an effulgent pair that usually shamed every other engine in sight when they turned up at Kings Cross; they were the so-called 'Royal Clauds', Class D16 or 'Claud Hamilton' 4-4-0s Nos 8783/7, which were painted LNER apple green and always kept dazzlingly clean, with every piece of metalwork gleaming, for Royal train haulage between London and Woolferton, station for the royal home at Sandringham.

Gresley had turned out his first Class N2 0-6-2T in 1920 and by 1923 the type was already in command of the Kings Cross inner suburban services, though a few of the earlier Class N1 hung about the area for the next two decades. The resilient N2's only serious LNER challenger until the eleventh-hour appearance of Thompson's Class L1 2-6-4T, was the ex-GE Class N7 0-6-2T. In 1925 Gresley decided to build a batch of N7s for the Kings Cross workings, but these smaller-wheeled engines were ill-matched to the quite tightly-timed, limited-stop trains that figured in the Kings Cross peak-hour schedules. Eventually the few N7s retained in the London area were concentrated at Hatfield to work the St Albans, Dunstable and Hertford branches, from some of which the N2s were barred because their high-pitched boilers made their stability suspect on sharp curves.

Extension of London Transport's Piccadilly Tube from Finsbury Park through Wood Green and Southgate to Cockfosters in 1932-3 drained off a lot of the Kings Cross inner suburban traffic, and more was taken off the LNER's hands with the Northern Line takeover of the High Barnet and Edgware branches in 1939-41. Until 1932 Finsbury Park was a very busy interchange between Kings Cross, Broad Street and Piccadilly trains, its platforms bustling with commuters and trains at the peak hour; many trains terminated or started there. In 1929, as P. N. Townend writes in his absorbing narrative of Kings Cross depot life, *Top Shed,* a Kings Cross N2 could cover nearly 250miles in a 20hr day from 6.11 to 1.02 next morning, working nine times in an out of London to Cuffley, Gordon Hill, Hertford, Potters Bar, New Barnet and High Barnet.

The N2 was carefully contoured to the limits of size and weight allowed over the former Metropolitan Railway Widened Lines, whereby some GN rush-hour inner suburban trains could work to and from the heart of the City at Moorgate. For these subterranean trips the London area N2s were equipped to condense their exhaust via the chunky external pipes that wound from their smokeboxes into their side tanks. The return journey from Moorgate always faced an N2 driver with one sticky moment, as the exit from the Widened Lines brought the train out of tunnel into Kings Cross platform 16 (now 14) on a tight curve that steepened to 1 in 37 in the platform itself. Often it needed several setbacks and a bone-crunching snatch at the train before the N2 could be coaxed away into the sulphurous murk of Gasworks Tunnel.

Of the suburban workings at the final LNER London terminal, Marylebone, there is little to remark, except that the ex-GC type Class A5 4-6-2Ts which dominated its local trains were the most graceful of the LNER's London commuter traffic engines. The atmosphere at Marylebone, even in the peaks, was sedate by comparison with that of Kings Cross, Fenchurch Street and Liverpool Street.

Top left: Condenser-fitted Class N2 0-6-2T No 4760 on a Gresley 'sit-up-and-beg' articulated suburban set approaches Potters Bar./*P Ransome-Wallis*

Centre left: One of the green-liveried 'Royal Clauds', Class D16/3 4-4-0 No 8787, on a Cambridge-Kings Cross train in 1932./*E R Wethersett: Ian Allan Library*

Bottom left: GC-type Class A5 4-6-2 No 5024 and typical Marylebone outer suburban train of 1938, climbing away from Rickmansworth./*Ian Allan Library*

Electrics, Diesels and Railcars

The North Eastern Railway had taken up electrification long before the LNER's formation. Like several other pre-1923 railways it had been savaged by turn-of-the-century tramway development — in this case Tyneside Tramways' new route from Gosforth to North Shields, which quickly drained the competing railway of nearly a third of its passengers — and reacted by electrifying.

In 1903-4 the North Tyneside loop from Newcastle Central out to Wallsend, Tynemouth, Whitley and back via Gosforth to Newcastle New Bridge Street was converted to 600V dc third-rail, together with the Riverside loop from Byker to Percy Main and a short section of the East Coast main line between Heaton Junction and Benton. Ancillary electrification of the Ponteland branch was planned but not pursued, and from 1929 this line was relegated to freight only, not to come back into passenger reckoning until the Tyne & Wear County Council wrote it into their 'Super-Tram' Metro network in the 1970s. In 1909-10 a short link was built between New Bridge Street and Manors, to allow circuit working from and back to Newcastle Central, though this was not practised until 1917, whereafter New Bridge Street was abandoned.

The NER at first operated the North Tyneside network with some distinctive clerestory-roof, open-saloon electric multiple-units, plus three self-propelled parcels cars, two of which could double as locomotives on a six-car set of adapted steam passenger stock at peak periods. A few of these inaugural units survived into LNER ownership, but nearly half the fleet was destroyed when fire ravaged the system's maintenance depot at Heaton in 1918. They were replaced by a new elliptical-roofed pattern of car in standard NER deep crimson lake livery, instead of the red and cream applied to the original stock.

In conjunction with the North Tyneside scheme the NER electrified Newcastle's short Quayside goods branch, an offshoot from the main line at Manors with gradients as stiff as 1 in 27. Except in tunnels the branch was equipped with overhead current supply, because its shunting operations would have made third rail a hazard to ground staff. Two small Bo-Bo electric locomotives were specially built for the branch and monopolised it until the current was switched off and the work handed over to diesels in 1964.

The NER dreamed of electrifying the East Coast main line between York and Newcastle. As a test-bed, it set out in 1913 to electrify from the West Durham coal concentration yard at Shildon to the Erimus yard between Thornaby and Middlesbrough, which had been laid out in 1908 to sort traffic for the Tees-side export quays and the area's iron and steelworks. Some 18 route- and 50 track-miles were converted to electric traction, in this case on the 1.5kV dc overhead system, an innovation for Britain. Electric operation was inaugurated in July 1, 1915, with a stud of 10 1,100hp Bo-Bo locomotives, but between the wars coal traffic slumped to a level that no longer justified the running costs of electric traction and the catenary was abandoned for steam in 1935. The 10 locomotives were stored for prospective use on the Manchester-Sheffield line, electrification of which was by then projected; one was in fact modified after the war for its new role, but BR decided the design was obsolescent and all 10 were scrapped without re-entering service.

Far more of a white elephant was the 1,800hp 2-Co-2 locomotive hopefully built by the NER's CME, Sir Vincent Raven, 1922. This was the prototype for the York-Newcastle scheme, but that never materialised. Apart from spasmodic tests in the Newport-Shildon area, the 2-Co-2 never earned a serious haulage penny from birth to death. BR scrapped it in 1949.

In 1934 the LNER set about electrifying the rest of the Tyneside commuter network and simultaneously renewed the North Tyneside equipment. On South Tyneside the conductor rail was threaded from Newcastle across the Tyne to Gateshead and via Jarrow and Tyne Dock to South Shields. A fleet of new-style multiple-units, marshalled from articulated twin-sets, was built for North Tyneside together with a pair of similar parcels cars; the newest North Tyneside sets were refurbished for the South Tyneside system; and the entire Tyneside stock was decked out in a new livery of blue and white. But in the 1960s the network went the same way as the Newport-Shildon electrification. So much off-peak traffic had drifted on to the roads that continuous electric working had become hopelessly unviable and in 1967 the conductor rail was de-energised; diesel multiple-units took over.

Down south, the LNER had put in hand electrification studies for the whole of the Liverpool Street and Kings Cross suburban networks as soon as it took over. From 1923 to 1925 sporadic Parliamentary questions elicited a stock reply that the matter was still under active study, after which public opinion was quiescent until the LNER revived the schemes in 1930. In the end the LNER Board was defeated by the high

Top: Tyneside suburban electrification: a set of the final North Eastern Railway North Tyneside electric multiple-unit stock in LNER blue-and-white livery, after transfer to the South Tyneside lines, entering Newcastle Central from South Shields./*Ian Allan Library*

Above: A train of the LNER articulated-twin electric multiple-units for the North Tyneside lines, built in 1938.

capital cost, though it did not publicly concede the point until the early 1930s.

Salvation came in the 1933 formation of the London Passenger Transport Board with a remit to take over all the capital's Tube and underground lines and an encouragement to cooperate above ground with the 'Big Four' wherever inter-system connections existed or were possible. Soon afterwards, to get much-needed improvement of London's rail services on the move, the Government organised a pooling of LPTB and 'Big Four' London suburban revenue and provided for guaranteed loans to underwrite electrification. With this backing plans were laid to extend the LPTB Central Line, firest to a surface interchange with the LNER at a completely rebuilt Stratford station, then via Leyton and Leytonstone to a Tube takeover of the ex-GER Woodford and Ilford line, and from Leyton onwards the entire Loughton and Ongar branch.

This both eased the LNER's financial burden and its operating load into and out of Liverpool Street, particularly by mitigating congestion of the flat junctions between Bow Junction and Stratford. With so much commuter traffic disposed of underground the LNER could now cope with electrification of its own suburban services between Liverpool Street and Shenfield, and simplify their operation by a wholesale layout reorganisation. From the terminus out to Manor Park the former local and fast lines were switched, so that the new Shenfield electrics would take the east side of the layout, then between Manor Park and Ilford a flyover was erected to bring the slow lines back to their original site and ensure convenient access to Ilford depot and Gidea Park storage sidings. The war interrupted both schemes and although most of the civil engineering work had been finished by 1947 — the Ilford flyover, a priority to avoid station modification north of Ilford, was in fact ready in 1940 — the LNER had been buried before the electric service, at 1.5kV dc overhead, was publicly inaugurated in September, 1949.

Before then, however, another joint enterprise with the LPTB had come to fruition. From 1940 Class N2 0-6-2Ts no longer panted up the hills to High Barnet, then tinkled their easier way back to Finsbury Park. By the spring of 1939 the LBTB's Northern Line trains had come north from Archway to a rebuilt East Finchley station, and in the following April they displaced steam on the rest of the branch.

In the mid-1930s the LNER also embarked on a main-line electrification. In 1931 it had cooperated with the LMS to convert the jointly-owned Manchester South Junction & Altrincham residential line, to fend off menacing competition from buses. The MSJA electrification was the first in Britain to adopt the recommendations on future method of the Government-appointed Weir Committee issued in 1927, and to employ 1.5kV dc overhead current supply. In 1936 the LNER decided to electrify similarly the difficult, heavily coal-laden ex-GC route over the Pennines from Sheffield to Manchester, which reaches a 943ft summit above sea level at the eastern end of Woodhead Tunnel. Much had been accomplished by the outbreak of war, which pulled down the shutters on this scheme too, though the prototype mixed traffic electric locomotive, LNER No 6701, was completed in 1941. After the war it took until 1954 to finish the job, which was protracted because of belated realisation that the deteriorating single-line Woodhead Tunnels must be replaced by a brand new double-track bore at an extra cost of over £4 million.

After World War I road transport began to bleed the railways in earnest. By now the private car was in contention as well as the bus and tram, and the General Strike of 1926 encouraged its use to the extent that in two years the LNER's annual passenger carryings slumped by 47million. To try and regain lost rural ground the LNER took up a contemporary development of the pre-1923 steam rail-motor, the

Below: LNER No 6701, the 1941-built Manchester-Sheffield 1500V dc electrification prototype locomotive of what is today BR Class 76. After the end of World War II the prototype had a protracted evaluation on the Netherlands Railways pending completion of the British scheme, to mark which it was named *Tommy* — its nickname to Dutch railwaymen while abroad./*Cecil J Allen collection*

Right: Clayton steam railcar No 41.

Below right: Sentinel steam railcar *Nettle* on the Middlesbrough-Whitby-Scarborough coast line. It is liveried green and white.

self-contained passenger vehicle that either articulated a small, orthodox locomotive and coach or built the locomotive and passenger accommodation into one vehicle. The new variant was a self-contained railcar embodying a high-speed Sentinel geared engine powered by an automatically-fired, high-pressure water-tube boiler; the same power plant was used in steam road wagons of the period. It was cheap to run, though it tended to be expensive on maintenance, and it had a wide route availability. Its chief defect was inflexible capacity; a 100-125hp output could not cope with a conventional coach trailer at peak traffic periods.

Between 1925 and 1930 the LNER, keenest of all the 'Big Four' on the concept, acquired nearly 90 steam railcars, most of them built by Metro-Cammell on the Sentinel principle, but some from the Clayton Wagon Co. The latter were distinguished by slender coupling rods on the power bogie and an incongruous open coal bunker in front of the driving cab. The Clayton cars had all been scrapped by 1937, chiefly because the Clayton concern went into liquidation and spares were unobtainable; the Sentinel vehicles were longer-lived.

In 1928 Sentinel developed a six-cylinder, poppet-valve engine that markedly improved the railcars' power/weight ratio, but the vehicles' restricted seating

Above: Armstrong-Whitworth diesel-electric railcar *Lady Hamilton* and trailer made their debut in 1934.

Above right: This Armstrong-Whitworth 880hp diesel-electric locomotive was tested on the Newcastle-Berwick and Newcastle-Carlisle routes in 1933.

capacity still fretted the operators. A 1929 effort to surmount the problem with very lightweight four-wheel trailers was not conspicuously successful; only eight were built. So, in1930-2, five twin-engined 200hp cars were produced specifically for the railcars' most sharply graded routes and in 1930 an articulated twin-unit was turned out with a single 200hp engine. Named *Phenomena,* this last covered the switchback lines in the Scarborough and Whitby coastal areas.

At first the railcars were painted in a facsimile of the standard varnished teak, then for a period they matched the Tyneside electric units in red and cream, but for most of their career they were liveried white above and green below the waistline. The whole fleet was racily named after old stage-coaches — *Tally Ho, Red Rover, Chevy Chase, True Briton, Hark Forward, Flower of Yarrow,* etc — and each car had a panel in its saloon recounting the history of its predecessor, which also offered monetary rewards to any riders who could add to knowledge of the original road coach. The last steam railcar was scrapped in early

1948, but many of the 58 four-wheeled light shunting locomotives built around Sentinel engines lasted longer into the BR era.

The LNER was an oil-engined railcar pioneer. It had inherited from the Great Central a 90hp petrol-electric car built as early as 1912, which began its revenue-earning life in the London area, running between Marylebone and South Harrow, but subsequently retreated to service between Macclesfield and Bollington until 1935, when it was scrapped and superseded by a Sentinel steam railcar. Two more petrol-electric cars were operating in the North-East from 1923 to 1931.

By the 1930s the diesel engine was making its mark and in 1932 the LNER took in for test at Middlesbrough a 250hp six-cylinder engine diesel-electric car built by Armstrong Whitworth, and in 1933 a light 95hp railbus by the same firm. The latter was not pursued, but in 1934 the LNER purchased the 250hp prototype and two further cars for stock, plus trailers; they were embellished with names — *Tyneside Venturer, Lady Hamilton* and *Northumbrian* — and put to work on second-rank express services in the North-East.

Liveried an attractive blue and cream, *Lady Hamilton* operated from Hull to Pontefract, Selby and York, *Tyneside Venturer* from Middlesbrough to Scarborough and *Northumbrian* from Leeds to Harrogate and York. By the end of the decade, when *Northumbrian* had also been sent to Hull, the cars were in perpetual mechanical trouble and all were withdrawn in 1939, though they were not broken up until the war's end.

Various diesel locomotives built speculatively by private industry were given trials, starting as early as 1924 with a little 20ton, 60hp Austrian-built 0-4-0 that was given a fling on the GE line and with coupled wheels of a tiny 2ft 9⅞in diameter took just under 6hr to trundle four coaches from Tottenham to Cambridge. But it was not until shortly before nationalisation that the LNER invested in its own diesel-electric shunters.

The company was now set to embark on main-line dieselisation. The immediate post-war scarcity of good steam coal coupled with an enthusiastic first-hand report on US railroad dieselisation by one of its chief officers persuaded the Board in 1947 to authorise purchase of 25 1,600hp diesel- electric main-line locomotives for the East Coast Route, but within months the newly-formed Railway Executive's mechanical chief had opted to prolong steam's life with a new range of standard classes. So the LNER scheme was aborted, becoming just a footnote to British traction history.

Freight Services

At the birth of the LNER Britain was living off coal to a much greater extent than today, not merely fuelling its homes and industries with it, but exporting it in millions of tons every year. The LNER alone was shifting over 100million tons of coal in 1923, more than half the entire National Coal Board output in the late 1970s. That load, though, was to decline drastically as the 1920s slithered into depression and unemployment, with a dismal effect on LNER finances.

The North Eastern Railway handed to the new-born LNER the biggest coal wagon fleet owned by any 1923 company, because it handled the output of its Durham, Northumberland and Yorkshire pits entirely in its own vehicles. A large part of the heavy flow from the Midlands coalfields up the GN and GE main lines to London and the south moved in privately-owned merchants' wagons, which, when fairly fresh from the paintshop, enlivened the coal drags trundling past my 1930s vantage point in Hadley Wood with colour, like the well-remembered orange of J. R. Wood and the various reds of some other factors.

Coping with the contrasted needs of bulk export shippers and small-town merchants led the NER to develop some aspects of modern merry-go-round techniques well before World War I. For most of the LNER era its mineral trains in the North-East were still characterised by ex-NER tapered-body hopper wagons that could be overhead-loaded with ore or coal and quickly emptied through bottom doors. The NER laid out many of its wayside goods yards with miniature versions of the huge incline-approached staiths at its ports, so that these wagons were adaptable to both bulk industrial hauls and wagonload domestic coal movement. However, destination

Below: Ex-NER Class J26 0-6-0 No 525 heads south from York with a load of typical NER wooden-bodied coal hopper wagons./*Real Photographs*

Right: A New England-Ferme Park coal train powered by Gresley Class O3 2-8-0 No 3468 south of Potters Bar Tunnel./*Real Photographs*

Below right: Booster-fitted Class P1 2-8-2 No 2393 emerges from Hadley Wood South Tunnel with a New England-Ferme Park coal train./*Ian Allan Library*

L N E R
2393

facilities were far from standard and the NER had also to cater for side- or end-door unloading, or for bodily up-ending in tipplers.

The NER was years ahead of the rest of the country in building high-capacity mineral wagons, too. As early as 1902 it was turning out 20ton-capacity four-wheelers, when other companies could carry no more than 10 or 12 tons per vehicle. And within that first decade it was adding to its stock 30ton-capacity bogie hoppers and bogie bolster wagons for its steel traffic from Consett and Tees-side, to supersede the close-coupled sets of two or three four-wheelers that were previously the only recourse for lengthy steel plates and sections. Both GNR and NER disposed of 40ft-long bogie well wagons for bulky industrial castings and machinery.

It was the GNR, though, that handed the LNER the most advanced wagons — some 50ton-capacity bogie wagons, each able to take 20,000 bricks, designed by Gresley for the important brickfield traffic from the Peterborough area. As they were equipped with continuous brake, these elegant wagons were often marshalled at the front of the heavy coal trains from Peterborough's New England yards to London's Ferme Park yard, near Hornsey.

New England was a key concentration point for assembly of Midlands coal into massive trains for the south, which would be dispersed to destination in short-haul trains from Ferme Park. The standard gross loading of these coal trains was 1000tons and by the early 1930s the Gresley 2-8-0s were being timed to wheel them from New England to Ferme Park at an average of 26mph, which was no mean specification for a loose-coupled train in those days.

It was for these New England-Ferme Park trains that in 1925 Gresley put his Pacific boiler on a three-cylinder 2-8-2, the Class P1, and gave it extra punch with an auxiliary engine, or booster, to drive the trailing axle within a low speed range and so enhance the starting tractive effort. Each of the Pls, Nos 2393/4, could comfortably move 100wagon trains of 1600 tons. But they were ahead of their time. Signalling and layouts were too cramped: at Hornsey, for instance, the 100wagon trains had to be split up for marshalling before they left the main line as the yard reception

Below: Ferme Park yards looking south, with a Class O3 2-8-0 leaving on coal empties. Off main running lines the LNER often economised in signal gantries by mounting splitting signals for divergences ahead vertically on one post, as here: the topmost signal was for the furthest left, the bottom for the furthest right turnout./*Ian Allan Library*

Below right: Specimen LNER bogie wagons: from top to bottom, for steel, sulphate and fish respectively.

tracks could not cope with them intact. So the 2-8-2s were put out to grass in the late 1930s and did little that realised their full potential in their last years before scrapping in 1945 — the first Gresley design, ironically, to be extinguished.

Unexpectedly, it was the freight business in former Great Eastern territory that most warmed the LNER management's hearts as recession from the immediate post-war boom dipped carryings elsewhere on the system. By 1925 ex-GE line freight had risen 20 per cent above its pre-1914 level, largely because sugar beet had become a staple East Anglian crop. This was tending to split the railway at its operational seams. So it was that East Anglia acquired Britain's most advanced post-war marshalling yard, at Whitemoor, near March in Cambridgeshire. Begun in 1925 and finished four years later, the down yard was the first in the country to employ remotely-controlled rail-brakes for graduated deceleration of wagons rolling off the hump into the sorting sidings. It was also the first to have all its points electrically operated from the control cabin, not manhandled individually by ground staff. The up yard was similarly equipped by 1933. Besides concentrating and forwarding agricultural traffic to and from East Anglia, Whitemoor was the counterpart of New England in assembling into East and North-East London trainloads coal that was funnelled up the GN-GE Joint line from Yorkshire pits

and across country via Peterborough from Midland collieries.

Another consequence of this upsurge of freight business in the LNER's Southern Area was the purchase from the War Department's Disposals Board between 1924 and 1929 of 273 war surplus 2-8-0s of J. G. Robinson's GCR design. This rugged type had been first choice for Army railway units in the 1914-18 war theatres and a vast number had been built for Government use — so vast that a great many went straight into mothballs and were almost factory-fresh when the LNER took them over. Most were distributed between March and Doncaster sheds, at each end of the GN/GE Joint line.

Throughout the 1920s the LNER was extensively building new wagons, particularly high-capacity coal wagons and bogie bolsters for the North-East's coal and engineering products. Even so, in early BR days one could still come across the odd and by then ramshackle wooden wagon on which a faded 'GC', 'GN' or 'GE' had emerged from under peeling paint. By 1935, however, new coal wagons were all-steel.

The GNR had been in the van of merchandise freight train acceleration — it claimed to have been the first railway in Britain to run a fully braked goods train — and the LNER maintained the tradition. The status of the celebrated 'Scotch Goods' was as much as that of passenger expresses. This was the braked train that had pulled out of Kings Cross between 3.25 and 3.40 every afternoon since 1897. By 1932, taking 13hr 38min for the 440 miles to Glasgow, it was the flagship of the LNER's fleet of 119 'No.1 fully braked' category freights, conveying perishable as well as manufactured goods, all of which promised next-day delivery. But perhaps the outstanding performance was that of the Aberdeen-Kings Cross freight that was scheduled to run the whole 523 miles of its itinerary at an average of 44mph. Other timetabled 'No.1' averages of 1932 were London: (Clarence Yard)-Edinburgh, 389miles at 41.2mph average; Newcastle to Liverpool, 196miles at 39.9mph average; Glasgow to Marylebone, 470miles at 37.7mph; Kings Cross to Leeds, 186miles at 35.5mph average; and Kings Cross to Manchester, 210miles at 32.3mph average. Tightly timed, too, were the afternoon and evening express braked fish trains that fanned out from Mallaig, Aberdeen, Hull and Grimsby to London, South Wales via Banbury, the Midlands and the North-West; they used to say at Lincoln you could check the Cathedral clock against the precision timekeeping of the Grimsby-Banbury evening train, the working of which was treated as reverently as that of an express passenger train. Today, unhappily, their traffic has been wholly squandered to road transport. The 'No.2 partially braked' merchandise freights were no slouches either.

At 60mph the 'No.1' trains had their standard 12ft-wheelbase brake-vans bucking and reeling like one of those little French Citroen cars hard-driven on a country road. Guards rebelled and Gresley set about mollifying them. First he tried weighting a standard brake-van with a reinforced concrete superstructure, but that made the inside so cold and damp that guards blacked the vehicle (incidentally the concrete idea was exhumed in 1940 as a way of saving scarce wood and steel, but rejected as adding too much to train weight). Gresley's eventual solution was to lengthen the brakevan wheelbase to 16ft, but not the superstructure, which only partially filled the frame floor, like the upper works of a ship: hence the popular description of the vans as 'battleships'. In its essentials the Gresley concept was standardised for the whole BR system after nationalisation. Another development connected with the spread of fast freight service was the construction from 1930 onwards of specialised four-wheel flat wagons for container traffic.

Some spectacular wagons were built for special traffics. Outstanding was a five-wagon set to carry very bulky machinery that was turned out in 1929. Its centrepiece was a very deep well wagon, with two flat wagons on each flank on to which some of the load's weight could be transferred by cantilever girders; the whole outfit was 226ft long, was carried on 56 wheels and could take a load of 150tons. By 1939, though, Gresley had devised a single well wagon, mounted on four six-wheel bogies, that on its own could carry 120tons (its own weight was 89 tons) and a smaller 12-wheeler capable of taking 50tons.

Although sharpening road competition severely dented the LNER's freight carryings in the 1930s, several important schemes were put in hand principally to benefit the freight business. Notable among them were the four-tracking of the East Coast main line between York and Northallerton, and new yards at Mottram and at Hull, discussed in the next chapter. By the outbreak of war modernisation had reduced the wagon stock by over 10 per cent compared with 1923 but with a concurrent increase in total carrying capacity; and the company could deploy over 50,000 wagons with continuous brakes for its express merchandise freight services.

Above: Britain's first mechanised marshalling yard, Whitemoor Down, seen from the hump, with the control cabin and retarders in the foreground.

Above right: Robinson ex-GC Class O4 2-8-0 No 6558 emerges from Peascliffe Tunnel, near Grantham, with an up coal train in 1946./*Ian Allan Library*

Right: Class V2 2-6-2 No 4789 at the head of an East Coast main line brake-fitted freight in the 1930s./*Ian Allan Library*

No 6558

No 4789

Improving the System

Strapped for cash though it was for most of its life, the LNER managed some worthwhile improvements of the way and works — or 'infrastructure' in contemporary jargon — that it inherited. Some were meaningful developments for the future of British railways generally.

Two significant schemes affecting the East Coast main line were in progress when the LNER took over. One was extension of the GN's London suburban Wood Green-Cuffley branch northward to rejoin the main line at Stevenage in a burrowing junction, thereby establishing the invaluable Hertford loop around the Welwyn Viaduct double-track bottleneck. This new line, which involved boring the 2,684yd-long Ponsbourne Tunnel, one of the LNER's longest, was opened to passenger traffic on June 2, 1924. At the same time the first exercises to close gaps in four-tracking where widening was economically manageable were active at Huntingdon and Peterborough, where additional bridges were being thrown over the Ouse and Nene rivers.

Back in London, the operating capacity of Kings Cross had been enlarged, and not before time. The first step had been taken in 1922 by the GNR, which was obliged to order a new 70ft turntable for the terminus engine yard to accommodate Gresley's Pacifics; in their earliest days they had to be sent right out to Hornsey to turn. The new turntable was eventually delivered in 1924 and installed hard by the mouth of Gasworks Tunnel. The engine yard was shifted to its perimeter; this vacated an area between the main station and the down line climbing up from the Metropolitan Widened Lines, which was now filled with two extra Suburban Station platforms, Nos. 14 and 15. Two years later an additional island platform, Nos 7 and 8, was erected in the down side of the main station, appropriating what had previously been carriage storage sidings.

Another London suburban development of late 1925 was the LNER's access to Watford. This was one more pre-Grouping inheritance. Prior to World War I, in 1912, the Metropolitan and GC companies had jointly obtained powers to project a branch from a triangular junction with their main line below Rickmansworth into the developing residential area on the western side of Watford. The job had not been

Below: The down side of Kings Cross main station when carriage roads filled the centre of the area: an early post-Grouping photo with ex-GC Class B3 4-6-0 No 1164 *Earl Beatty* (yet to receive its LNER number 6164) ready to leave with the Harrogate Pullman./*F R Hebron*

LNER 1930s-style architecture at Shenfield, on the GE line: (*top right*) the old station in 1931; and (*centre right*) the new station erected during the big four-tracking scheme./*Ian Allan Library*

Bottom right: Otterington, one of the neat new stations constructed during the widening between York and Thirsk./*Ian Allan Library*

BOVRIL

started until 1922 and in 1923, of course, the LNER assumed the GC interest. The new line was opened flamboyantly with about 70 trains each day daily, roughly half Metropolitan and half LNER to and from Marylebone.

In 1926 Welwyn Garden City station was opened and there was considerable modernisation at Cambridge. The university city station's bi-directional through platform, intersected by a scissors crossover connection with the adjoining through line so that one half can serve down trains, the other up, was further lengthened. The whole layout was remodelled to improve the up and down goods yards, and the five mechanical signalboxes were dismantled in favour of a new two-signalbox installation, power-controlling semaphore signals and points electrically from miniature lever frames. Though the Cambridge scheme employed semaphores, by this time the LNER was already applying three-aspect colour-lights to sections of the East Coast main line.

Today's Berwick-on-Tweed station dates from 1927. The previous station was cramped and nastily curved where the main line threaded the platforms. The curve could not be eliminated, but it was greatly eased by spreading the main line around one new, wide and gently arced island platform, though to make room for this relief lines round the back of the station had to be sacrificed.

To catch up with Clacton's rapid 20th Century development an imposing new station was bestowed on the town in 1929; the original two island-platform layout was retained, but the platforms were substantially widened, realigned and lengthened, and the cramped old wooden offices were replaced by a big new complex with a palated facade. Clacton was so taken with its new facility that in 1933 the Clacton pier owners vainly offered to put up £10,000 towards purchase of German 'Fliegende Hamburger'-type diesel railcars for the Liverpool Street service.

The biggest GE Line innovation of 1929, though, was the commissioning of the new mechanised up marshalling yard at Whitemoor, near March, as described in Chapter Eight. It relieved pressure on the congested interchange yards at Peterborough and diverted a great deal of southbound coal traffic from the East Coast main line to the Doncaster-Sleaford-Spalding route, to which some 50 refuge loops were added at 30 different locations in 1929-31.

There was new and seemingly more purposeful talk of London suburban electrification in 1930. Preparation of a scheme for an underground line from Liverpool Street to Ilford was announced and in opposing the London Electric Railway's plan to extend what is

Below: A key development in British signalling: the first entrance-exit, route-setting signalbox panel at Thirsk./*British Rail*

Resignalling at Edinburgh Waverley: (*right*) the miniature lever frame of the East box; and (*below right*) the West end, controlled by a similar installation, after resignalling, with Class P2 2-8-2 No 2004 *Mons Meg* leaving for Aberdeen./*E R Wethersett: Ian Allan Library*

now the LT Piccadilly Tube from Finsbury Park to Cockfosters the LNER exhumed its Kings Cross-Welwyn Garden City and Hertford electrification project, throwing in also the High Barnet, Alexandra Palace and Edgware branches. With the possibility of a Government Grant under the 1929 Development Act, which had been framed to stimulate new public works as a counter to the industrial slump, the GN scheme was more economically practicable than in the 1920s; the Welwyn and Hertford conversions were reckoned to cost £3.7 million, plus £650,000 to quadruple the three-tunnel, double-track section between New Barnet and Potters Bar. But at the end of the day, of course, it was the Piccadilly Tube scheme which the Government opted to support, and the LT Northern Line which took over the Barnet and Edgware branches.

However, the GE line operators were granted some relief by a widening of their outer suburban trackage. Dormitory growth in the Romford area was now intensive, but the Colchester main line's quadruple track stopped short of the station. First, then, Romford station was rebuilt with four platforms, a new two-island-platform station was erected at the budding suburb of Gidea Park, and four-tracking was carried through to new carriage sidings at Harold Wood. The only pity was that the constraints of site and layout rearrangement forced the curvature of the up main line round one Gidea Park island platform so tightly that a

Above: The original Woodhead Tunnel, on the Manchester-Sheffield route: on the left is Class O4 2-8-0 No 6349, while emerging from the tunnel is one of the Riddles ex-WD 2-8-0s which the LNER acquired after World War II./*British Rail*

Below right: The dream the LNER had to leave BR to realise — electrically hauled, a Manchester-Marylebone express crosses Dinting Viaduct en route to Sheffield behind the prototype LNER locomotive, by now BR No 26000 *Tommy*. Unhappily the line was threatened with closure in 1977 because of a severe slump in its coal traffic./*V Bamford*

60mph limit had to be imposed, curbing expresses on their descent of Brentwood bank. These improvements were completed in 1931.

Within months contracts were let for a still bolder extension of four-tracking from Harold Wood to Shenfield. This involved formidable civil engineering in widening the deep cutting between Brentwood bank and Ingrave summit, and sinking a burrowing junction at Shenfield to keep down Southend Victoria trains clear of main-line conflict; the project also provided for reconstructed stations at Harold Wood, Brentwood and Shenfield, the last-mentioned with five platforms.

A valuable widening in the Scottish Area had been approved in 1929 and was finished in 1932. The Arbroath-Montrose stretch of the Edinburgh-Aberdeen main line had been built as single track in 1881, then doubled only as far as Inverkeilor in 1897. Although it was decided to ignore about 2miles between Usan and Montrose because of the exceptionally heavy bridgework costs entailed, the rest of the 9¼miles was doubled; even that involved enlarging four substantial steel viaducts, three of three spans each and one of five.

In 1933 another important expansion of operating capacity was completed between York and Northallerton. At this time the double-track bottleneck over the Ouse at Skelton Bridge, just outside York, was left untouched, but beyond it additional tracks were laid for 2½ miles to link with the four tracks already existing from Beningbrough to Alne. A third track was installed on the down side from Alne to Pilmoor, then four-tracking was made continuous from Thirsk to Northallerton, where the slow lines were dropped into a burrowing junction with the Harrogate-Teesside line to avoid conflict between East Coast main-line traffic and some key freight flows on the level. The neat, new station buildings erected at stations affected by the widening evoked a lot of approving comment.

Associated with this scheme was a resignalling project of great significance for future British practice. For the first time in Britain the main-line potential of modern entrance-exit route signalling from thumb-switches superimposed on an illuminated track diagram was demonstrated in a new all-electric signalbox with route relay interlocking at Thirsk, with associated colour-light signals.

Resignalling predominated much of the modernisation news in the 1930s. Appropriately the first main centre to benefit was Kings Cross, where in 1932 the two mechanical boxes were superseded by a single all-electric cabin controlling colour-lights (the second stage of the changeover, incidentally, was one of those traumatic foul-ups that have the evening paper typesetters grabbing a 'Chaos!' headline by instinct). Four-aspect colour-lights with a double yellow were an innovation in the Gidea Park-Shenfield and Bethnal Green-Enfield resignalling of 1934. In 1936 Edinburgh Waverley acquired a new 227 miniature-lever, electric signalbox with train describers to take over control of the station's west end from five mechanical cabins, whereupon a similar installation was promptly ordered for the east end. And in 1937 the LNER finished the resignalling of Leeds New (now Leeds City) station with colour-lights controlled from two signalboxes, the East with a mixture of thumb-switch signal and mechanical lever point control, but the West with route relay interlocking and route-setting from a thumb-switch panel — the first application of this technique to a major city station.

Two important new marshalling yard schemes came to fruition in 1935. The ex-GC Woodhead main line over the Pennines was the LNER's only gateway from South Yorkshire to the industrial areas of Lancashire, the Cheshire Lines Committee system and the Wirral. The exchange yards for LMS-bound traffic at Guide Bridge and CLC-bound traffic at Godley had been quite outgrown by traffic increases, so in 1930 the LNER obtained powers to build a new yard at the nearest point with convenient space and terrain; this turned out to be Mottram, about 11 miles out of Manchester on the Woodhead route. The yard was opened in 1935 and soon afterwards Hull's new Inwards Yard, 2½miles long and with 30 sorting sidings capable of taking in all 2,700wagons from the power brake-equipped hump, was commissioned.

When Government guaranteed loans at low interest and over periods up to 16 years came on offer in 1935, as discussed in previous chapters, the LNER applied them to several pressing cases for operational improvement. East Anglia was one of the immediate beneficiaries. In the summer of 1936 the LNER announced a comprehensive reconstruction of Colchester station to enlarge the operating facilities and ease the irksome, 40mph-limited cúrve through the platforms. The Clacton branch was to be thoroughly rebuilt, the Southend branch to be equipped with colour-lights and have its intermediate station platforms lengthened. On the East Coast main line both Doncaster and York stations were to be remodelled (the latter with extra platforms outside the arched roof area) and resignalled with colour-lights. New reception tracks were to be installed to increase capacity at several locations south of Doncaster. The biggest commitment, though, was to electrification of the Manchester-Sheffield line and the associated freight feeder line from Wath up the Worsborough bank to the convergence at Penistone.

The war interrupted many of these projects. Some hint of its strains on the railway emerged in the earlier review of LNER motive power. Apart from the huge tonnages moved by scheduled train, in six years the LNER had to lay on over 127,000 special trains for troops, munitions and other Government traffic. Troop movement to populate the newly built East

Anglian bomber airfields alone demanded 460 specials, and every time a 1,000-bomber raid was mounted the LNER had to organise 28 trains of fuel and eight of bombs. More than three-quarters of the country's bomber bases, in fact, were located in LNER territory. More blitz damage was inflicted on the LNER than on any other railway, particularly by V2 rockets; the first V1 flying bomb to hit Britain plummeted on to the GE track between Bethnal Green and Stratford.

System improvement was not quite dormant during the war. As soon as the threat of war became oppressive, the Big Four had taken stock of their joint ability to handle the likely traffic flows a war machine would generate and decided that several new inter-system connections were essential. These were put in hand as quickly as possible, with the Government footing the bill.

One of the first touching the LNER was a new junction between the GN main line and the Tottenham & Hampstead Joint line at Haringay, completed in March, 1940; together with a simultaneous new link between the T&H and North London lines at Gospel Oak, it opened up an alternative route between the GN and GE lines and the SR should the direct cross-city Metropolitan Widened and East London lines be cut. Late in 1940 a spur was laid from the GN main line to the Cambridge-Bletchley-Oxford branch at Sandy; it was one of several such additions that in combination allowed traffic between the LNER and the South-East to circumnavigate London via Bedford, Bletchley, Claydon, Northolt Junction and Staines (in recent years more than one of the new links that created this route has been ripped up). Between York and Newcastle the 6 miles from Pilmoor to Thirsk were quadrupled, involving a total rebuilding of Thirsk station, and an emergency avoiding line was built to the west of Northallerton station in 1941; this last embodied a unique 'movable bridge' crossing of the single-line Hawes branch, necessary because the respective levels of the two lines did not leave enough clearance for a fixed structure.

In 1946 the LNER published an impressive programme of post-war modernisation. Some of its big projects, like the four-tracking and concomitant new tunnels on the GN main line between Hadley Wood and Potters Bar, and the extension of colour-light signalling from Doncaster all the way to Edinburgh, were eventually executed under BR. At least one, the merging of the two stations at Peterborough in one completely remodelled North station, was over 20 years in coming to pass; and the plan to rebuild the ex-GN Leeds Central station on modern lines was under BR superseded by concentration of the city centre's entire passenger traffic in a rejuvenated Leeds City station. A great deal of the plan, though, is still a pipe-dream, such as the complete reconstruction of Kings Cross, Cambridge, Norwich Thorpe and Grimsby Town stations.

But to the end of its days, to take the title of the booklet in which this post-war plan was promoted to the public, the LNER was as ever determined to drive *Forward*.

BR begins work on another unfulfilled LNER scheme, boring new tunnels at Hadley Wood to allow four-tracking thence to Potters Bar, in the London suburbs. Class V2 2-6-2 No 60983 emerges from the old North tunnel with a southbound stopping train./*British Rail*